Viva Studymates

Project Management

Viva Studymates

Project Management

How to plan and deliver a successful project

Vicky Billingham

Viva Books

New Delhi | Mumbai | Chennai | Kolkata | Bangalore | Hyderabad | Kochi | Guwahati

First Indian Edition 2010

VIVA BOOKS PRIVATE LIMITED

- 4737/23 Ansari Road, Daryaganj, New Delhi 110 002
  E-mail: vivadelhi@vivagroupindia.net, Tel. 42242200
- 76, Service Industries, Shirvane, Sector 1, Nerul, Navi Mumbai 400 706
  E-mail: vivamumbai@vivagroupindia.net, Tel. 27721273, 27721274
- Jamals Fazal Chambers, 26 Greams Road, Chennai 600 006
  E-mail: vivachennai@vivagroupindia.net, Tel. 28290304, 28294241
- B-103, Jindal Towers, 21/1A/3 Darga Road, Kolkata 700 017
  E-mail: vivakolkata@vivagroupindia.net, Tel. 22836381, 22816713
- 7, Sovereign Park Apartments, 56-58, K. R. Road, Basavanagudi, Bangalore 560 004
  E-mail: vivabangalore@vivagroupindia.net, Tel. 26607409, 26607410
- 101-102 Mughal Marc Apartments, 3-4-637 to 641, Narayanguda, Hyderabad 500 029
  E-mail: vivahyderabad@vivagroupindia.net, Tel. 27564481, 27564482
- Beevi Towers, First Floor, SRM Road, Kaloor, Kochi 682 018, Kerala
  E-mail: vivakochi@vivagroupindia.net, Tel: 0484-2403055, 2403056
- 232, GNB Road, Beside UCO Bank, Silpukhuri, Guwahati 781 003
  E-mail: vivaguwahati@vivagroupindia.net, Tel: 0361-2666386

www.vivagroupindia.com

Published by arrangement with
Studymates Limited
PO Box 2, Bishops Lydeard,
Somerset TA4 3YE,
United Kingdom

ISBN : 978-81-309-1308-7

Published by Vinod Vasishtha for Viva Books Private Limited, 4737/23, Ansari Road, Daryaganj, New Delhi-110 002. Printed and bound by Swan Press, New Delhi.

M0000 / M0201

Contents

List of illustrations

Foreword

It may seem a very grand way of opening the foreword to a book on Project Management but in my opinion a 'project' of one form or another lies behind all human endeavours. At one end of the spectrum, these 'projects' are on a global scale touching the lives of many people while at the other end they may be as simple as redecorating a back bedroom. Some end in disaster and some in triumph but all in some way bring change. As Vicky Billingham writes in her book, Project Management is all about effecting change.

In the past, the people leading such change may not have called what they were doing a 'project' or themselves 'Project Managers'. Whether it's an expedition to put an explorer ashore on a foreign land, a mission by scientists and engineers to put a man on the moon or a business need to put goods on a supermarket shelf, all are projects and behind all is a Project Manager.

One would assume that after years and years of such endeavour, with so many talented people undertaking such a vast number and wide variety of projects we would have learnt by now how to succeed in delivering them, on budget, on time, every time. Why is it then, that even today we read so often of spectacular project failures with projects overrunning on cost or time and when projects are completed, they don't deliver what was originally imagined of them?

Over the years, we have introduced formal Project Management methods, metrics, and qualifications with many books written on such subjects. However, for me these books all too often overlook that for a project to succeed, a Project Manager and a project team can't simply follow a sequence of rules and procedures. A project isn't just a succession of steps in a process and Project Management isn't the same as just following a recipe from a cookbook. The very fact that a project brings change means a Project Manager must manage creativity and apply a touch of art within the science.

All projects have that ingredient of uncertainty: people. Usually, very talented people who we then attempt to constrain into uniformity of planning, design, implementation etc. Inevitably, these people, be they customer, Project Manager or members of the project team bring their own approach to these disciplines. They will consider the experiences of their predecessors but then in a search for innovation will add something to that experience in order, as they see it, to address better the project goal they seek to achieve.

The challenge to the Project Manager is the management of all of this talent into a cohesive group of people all focused on the success of the project. One might say it's like herding cats, but I would rather liken the role of the Project Manager to a conductor of an orchestra, the customer being the 'audience' and each of the project members a different 'musician'. In order to delight his 'audience', the Project Manager must conduct his 'musicians' to bring the best out of each individual performance but in such a way that the whole orchestra keeps to the rhythm and beat of the music or 'project plan'. However, the task of the Project Manager is even harder than that of the conductor. Whereas the conductor of an orchestra can rehearse his musicians before performing for his audience, a Project Manager must achieve success on the first and only performance and with the 'audience' rewriting the music and sometimes seeking to play one or two of the instruments!

Why will buying and reading this book by Vicky Billingham make a difference to those involved in Project Management? As one would expect, in this book one will find lots of good information on the processes of Project Management. However, because Vicky knows that real people manage projects she includes practical handy hints and learning points based on her experience as a Project Manager. Vicky then structures all of this information well, allowing the reader to follow the book in sequence if they are taking on Project Management for the first time, while offering the more experienced Project Manager the opportunity, on those occasions when they may need to 'brush up' on a few areas, to easily refer to specific chapters in the book.

Throughout the book Vicky never neglects the human element in the art of Project Management. Whether it's quotes from the famous to remind us that Project Management is something of an ancient art and to encourage today's Project Managers to success, or the 'Diary of a Project Manager' which brings to life the doubt, worry and sense of achievement that all those who have managed projects will recognise immediately.

Vicky's book helps a Project Manager understand that the role is more than just managing process and activity. It is the management of people, be that the customer, the members of the project team or themselves!

Who, you might ask, am I to offer such plaudits on this book? Well, I have been involved in the delivery of projects as a team member, Project Manager, and Project Director for nigh on 30 years now and for part of that time, I worked alongside Vicky herself. In this book Vicky makes reference to Rudyard Kipling, and I too can quote him, as I personally have met with project "Triumphs and Disasters" and like Kipling, I hope to " treat those two impostors just the same", in that I learnt from both.

Over those 30 years, I have experience of a wide range of projects, including space programmes, communications systems, voting systems, systems to help pay people and systems to make sure people pay for things they buy. I was even involved in one of the projects Vicky mentions in this book, that of the Millennium Dome. Thankfully, the element I was responsible for did work to the paying public's satisfaction and was completed to budget. Given that we were up against an immovable deadline of the end of the Millennium, we managed to complete it on time too. Nevertheless, even with all this experience behind me, reading Vicky's book even reminded me of a few things on Project Management that had faded from memory. For example, all too often Project Managers see only the negative risk to their project and overlook those risks which are positive and thus deny themselves the opportunity to gain advantage by exploiting successfully such risk.

Regardless of how many years one may have behind them in Project Management, nor how much one has learnt along the way, a clearly structured book, containing sound facts but written from the perspective of experience and which brings out the people side of Project Management, is a valuable asset to be drawn upon time and time again.

Vicky Billingham has written such a book.

Harry Watson
Director
IFS Defence Ltd

Preface

This book was written in response to a need expressed to me by many delegates on Project Management training courses that I have delivered. There are many books on Project Management available, but none that seems to provide a practical guide for those wanting to move their careers into Project Management, or for Project Managers needing a quick reference to the essential elements involved. Also, there seems to be an absence of books taking a hands-on approach and asking the readers to apply their learning and understanding as they make progress.

I can understand why. Project Management is a generic topic, a common business skill for which the details and terminology vary widely between industries and organisations. Writing a book that is generic but useful, and based on common sense, yet at the same time informative, is not an easy task.

I hope this book helps you whatever your need. I fervently believe that Project Management is simply the organised and structured application of common sense, made trickier by the complexity and size of projects. But it remains common sense, however you look at it.

How to use this book

You can use this book in different ways; you can dip into it to find an answer to a specific problem, or you can read it cover-to-cover performing all of the practical exercises in order to familiarise yourself thoroughly with Project Management.

This book focuses the reader on the practical aspects of developing a Project Management Plan (PMP). The Project Management Plan is the complete definition of how the project will be executed. Each chapter of this book covers a different element of Project Management, and after each topic you will be asked to produce an element of the Project Management Plan for a Case Study project, which is described in Appendix A. By the end of this book you will have produced a full Project Management Plan, and you will be able to compare it with the sample one in Appendix B. Yours will undoubtedly look different from the one in Appendix B, but you will understand enough about these topics by that point to know whether or not any differences are significant.

Towards the end of each chapter are some multiple-choice questions that test what you have learnt. The answers to these questions can be found in Appendix C. This also has the added benefit of preparing you for the APM (Association of Project Management) Introductory Certificate examination. This is a one-hour multiple-choice examination on the fundamentals of Project Management, and provides a useful foundation for progressing to further Project Management qualifications. For more information on this examination, see the APM website referenced in Appendix D. This appendix contains a list of useful websites and further reading, for more research and development in your Project Management career.

You can get further support through my website (www.projectivity.co.uk). Just follow the links to test yourself using the on-line multiple-choice questions, and download templates for the key project management documents.

Whilst you are working through the book, if you need to check the meaning of a particular term, refer to the Glossary which follows Appendix D.

I realise that some people may perceive that a book on Project Management could be rather dry; I believe that actually it is potentially good fun and highly rewarding. To show this, throughout the book I have used real-life examples, and at the end of each chapter is an extract from the Project Manager's Diary. This diary is a fictional look at what might have happened during the Case Study project, and brings some of the key points from the chapter together in a light-hearted way.

Trademarks

Nomenclature

Throughout this book where the masculine form is used, it implies both the masculine and the feminine form.

Acknowledgements

Figure 7.1 (what the user wanted) is reproduced with kind permission of Robelle Solutions Inc.

Good Project Managers ensure they have a good team around them. My team was easy to find (and highly cost-effective) because my family all have relevant industry and academic experience. I would like to thank the following people: Philip Keevil, whose unstinting enthusiasm for this project and brilliant lateral thinking were infectious and motivating; Joan Keevil, whose ability to spot typographical and grammatical errors is second to none; Andrew Keevil, who brought valuable business experience into the mix; and Ruth Cleaver and Jax Aspden for their help in checking that the contents were comprehensible to those with no previous Project Management experience. Jamie provided excellent support and intuitive tea-making, and my husband Nigel produced all of the diagrams, reviewed and re-formatted tirelessly, and was an invaluable sounding-board and positive mentor throughout.

Vicky Billingham
vicky.billingham@studymates.co.uk

1 Definition of a project: Know where you're going before you start

This chapter explains what is meant by Project Management. It defines what we mean by a project, and what the key objectives of a Project Manager are, in delivering a successful project. The concept of managing groups of projects, known as programmes or portfolios, is introduced. The chapter divides a project life cycle into phases, and explains the relevant outputs from each phase, in particular the Project Management Plan (PMP). The importance of external factors that may affect the project is also explained.

- Why do we regularly hear about projects that are significantly delayed?
- Why do some projects cost many times more than their original budget?
- Why do some projects fail to deliver what was intended in the first place?
- What are the secrets of successful Project Management?

Consider examples of projects like the building of Wembley Stadium, the Scottish Parliament and the Millenium Dome. All of these projects suffered major problems.

Then consider the Millau Viaduct project—the building of the world's tallest viaduct. The viaduct was named after Millau, a small town in the middle of the Tarn Valley in south west France. The project finished on time, within cost and to an accuracy of 99.999%. It spans 2.5 kilometres, but when the two halves of the bridge, which were curved, were pushed together across the valley, they were aligned to within 1 mm!

So what are the important aspects of managing a project that make it successful? Years of study and anecdotal evidence point to one important fact: success doesn't rely on one particular aspect, but on a combination of factors working together. A successful Project Manager juggles all of the important components of a project, keeping them all on track throughout.

Another often-quoted belief is that Project Management is just structured common sense. This is (for the most part) true, especially when the project is small. But when a project is large or complex, you definitely need a method to help you manage the many different aspects successfully. This book suggests that the best way to maximise your chance of success is to produce a Project Management Plan (PMP) for the project. The PMP defines everything about the project before the technical work is started, and is used to monitor progress until the project is completed.

1.1 What is a project?

How do you decide that something is a project as opposed to an ordinary, day-to-day task?

A project is a one-off set of tasks which deliver a change. For example, replacing a computer system in an organisation will usually effect a large change to the users of that system. Work that is not project-based is often referred to as 'BAU' (Business as Usual).

BAU is the operational work that keeps a business running, such as opening the post, managing the accounts and paying invoices. Whilst small tasks can be managed as projects, they are often just part of someone's 'day job' and are therefore more likely to be BAU. It is sometimes thought that the main factor in deciding whether something should be treated as a project is the size of the task, but some non-project tasks can be very large, and some projects may be fairly small but have a large impact (e.g., cultural change projects).

Projects use a temporary organisation structure to deliver the results, whereas BAU is normally undertaken by a permanent team. So once the project is complete, the team will disband and go on to the next project possibly working with different people. A project always has a defined goal and a defined end, whereas BAU is ongoing and its goal is to keep the business running. Because projects are unique, they are more risky than normal business operations, which use tried and tested methods.

Project	BAU
unique	repetitive
delivers a change	keeps the business running
temporary organisation structure	permanent organisation structure
defined goal	continuation of business
start, middle and end	ongoing, no clear end
needs a project plan	no plan necessary, may have a process definition

Figure 1.1: Projects vs BAU.

Centralised functions like accountancy are not usually involved in project work. Accountants, Human Resources (HR) advisors and receptionists, for example, have day-to-day activities that they carry out repetitively working to the same set of objectives. To use an everyday example, you might choose to treat the re-decoration of a room in your house as a project, whereas a trip to the supermarket is BAU. An organisation would not treat carrying out staff appraisals as a project (they are on-going and repetitive throughout a person's career) but they might treat changes to the staff appraisal process as a project (a one-off development with a defined end).

Centralised functions may get involved with projects on an ad-hoc basis, when a project needs someone from the 'business' to advise on some aspect of the project, such as requirements or acceptance testing, but usually they are the recipients of the project outputs. So the HR department might advise on the requirements of the new staff appraisal process, will probably approve the project outputs, and will be the users of the project outputs.

1.2 Project objectives

Ultimately the measure of success of a project is the extent to which the results of the project bring the planned benefits to the organisation. So if a project to make changes to the staff appraisal process is undertaken, the organisation will be looking at the long-term effects of the new process and how they benefit the organisation. For example, this may result in reduced staff turnover in the next five years, and therefore this would be a project benefit. These benefits need to be clearly defined in the Business Case, which is included in the PMP.

At the close of the project, we cannot measure the long-term benefits to the organisation. The three measures of success at this time are time, cost and quality:

- Did we complete the project within the planned timescale?
- Did we remain within the project budget?
- Did we deliver the required quality and the required functionality?

These three objectives are often expressed in this form:

Figure 1.2: The three project objectives.

Imagine that the sides of this triangle can stretch. At each apex of the triangle is one of the three objectives. When one of these objectives is impacted, so are the other two. So for example, if you are halfway through the project and the customer suddenly demands more work, i.e., they require more functionality, then you would, quite naturally, respond with a request for more time and money to complete the job. If the customer changed his mind about the deadline, and wanted the project completed earlier, you might argue for more money to pay overtime or a reduction in the scope of the project, or both. And if the customer suddenly altered the budget for the work, again you might ask for a reduction in scope and this would alter the timescale as well.

It is important to note that these three constraints are very rarely of equal importance in a project. Most projects have one or two of these factors being more significant than the others. For instance, if you were managing the project to deliver the London 2012 Olympic Games, time would be the most important factor, as this is the one that cannot be sacrificed in order to meet the other targets, whatever the situation is. We may spend more money than planned, or deliver to a reduced quality, in order to meet the immovable time constraint. Quality is usually the most important factor in projects involving human safety, such as construction projects. These may overrun in terms of time and cost in order to meet safety standards. Cost will be the most important one of the three where the customer has an absolute limit on the budget. Sometimes customers will ask, "What can we have for £2 million?"

So the success of the Project Manager's role can be measured in terms of meeting these three objectives at the end of the project. And it could be said that these are the things that the Project Manager is 'juggling' throughout the project. But clearly measuring the achievement of these objectives cannot be done only at the end, for then it is too late to have changed anything about the project which might have improved the chances of success. So these three objectives need to be broken down into smaller objectives that can be measured along the way, so that we know where we are in terms of money spent, time taken and quality delivered throughout the project. Of primary importance, the project plan will contain the planned spend at milestones throughout the project, so that we can compare the actual expenditure at these points.

> "It must be considered that there is nothing more difficult to carry out, nor more doubtful of success, nor more dangerous to handle than to initiate a new order of things."
> Machiavelli, Italian statesman and philosopher

1.3 Programmes and portfolios

Programmes and portfolios are both groups of projects. In programmes, the projects are all part of the same overall business goal, whereas in portfolios the projects are not connected in terms of their goals, but are managed in a portfolio for reasons of convenience, such as all of the projects using the same pool of resources.

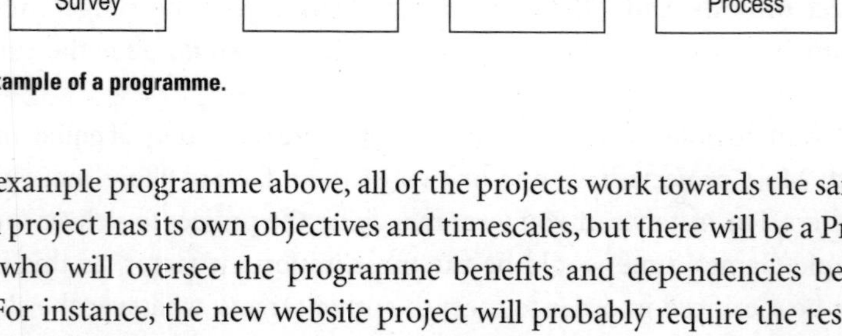

Figure 1.3: Example of a programme.

In the example programme above, all of the projects work towards the same overall goal. Each project has its own objectives and timescales, but there will be a Programme Manager who will oversee the programme benefits and dependencies between the projects. For instance, the new website project will probably require the results of the customer survey project in order to decide what should be included in the new website.

In the diagram below, which is an example of a portfolio, there are four projects currently undertaken by the IT department. They do not work towards the same goal but are managed as a unit as they use the same pool of IT resource. The IT department manager works as the Portfolio Manager and can move resources between the projects to the best effect. The IT portfolio represents a cost centre in the organisation.

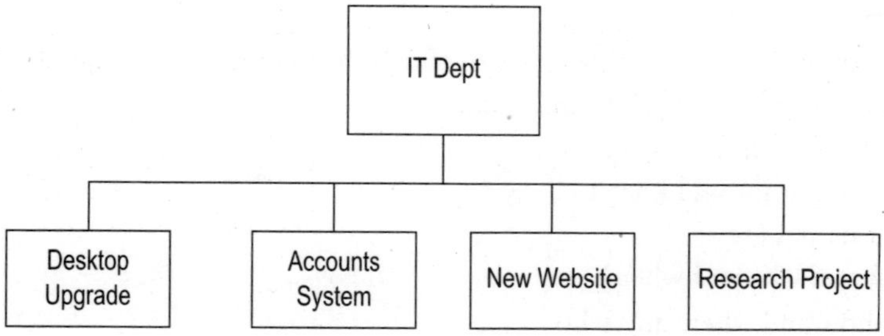

Figure 1.4: Example of a portfolio.

1.4 Project life cycle

A project is broken down into a life cycle of four main phases. This helps to define what needs to be done in terms of managing the project, decisions that need to be made and documents that need to be produced and approved. The life cycle phases are as follows:

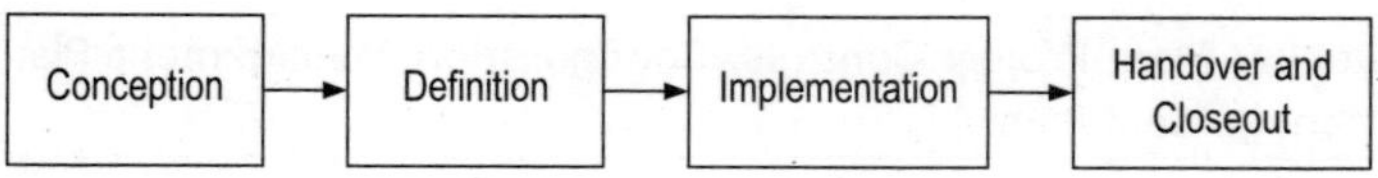

Figure 1.5: The project life cycle.

Conception

The Conception phase is where the need for the project is established and documented in the Business Case (see the next chapter for more details of this). It is a fairly short phase. It looks only at the decision about the project's viability, rather than defining how the project will run or actually developing any of the project's products.

If you know that you are definitely going to carry out the project, for example, if the project is needed to keep up with changes in legislation, you might question whether the Conception phase is really required. But due to the significance of the other benefits of this phase—the identification of major risks, an outline view of cost and time, and the seeking of approval to continue to the next phase—it is vital. The act of seeking approval to continue also confirms the ownership of the project by the Project Board.

Getting approval to progress on to the next phase can be achieved through the approval of a Definition Phase Plan by the Project Board. This will list the activities of the Definition phase, along with the time and cost for that phase. It is not always necessary to produce a Definition Phase Plan but it can be useful in setting the expectations of the Project Board. Otherwise the Project Board may assume that the Definition phase is short and fairly cheap to carry out.

If you are a supplier, you may not be involved in the Conception phase. The customer may have independently written his own Business Case before engaging with any suppliers. And you may not even see your customer's Business Case as this may be considered to be confidential.

Definition

A useful interpretation of this phase of the project comes from a quote by Rudyard Kipling in his poem *The Elephant's Child*:

"I keep six honest serving-men
They taught me all I knew;
Their names are
What and why and when
And how and where and who"

Definition is all about putting together a Project Management Plan (PMP) which covers all of the areas of a project that require planning and definition. This will then be followed by approval of the PMP before the project's technical work can start.

The work in this phase will take much longer and require more effort than Conception. We can relate the contents of the PMP to Kipling's six serving-men:

What	Project scope and requirements specification
Why	Business Case
When	Project Plan
How	Quality Plan, Project Controls, Configuration Management Plan, Change Management Plan
Where	Where in the plan? Any geographical constraints?
Who	Project Organisation Structure, Stakeholder Mgt Plan/Communication Plan

Project scope and requirements specification is concerned with what the project entails and the required specifications of the products that the project will develop. Chapter 3 covers this topic in detail. Chapter 3 will also cover the 'when', in terms of the Project Plan. **The Project Plan** refers to the plan of the major activities of the project, set against a timescale. Often this is produced by a specialist software planning tool, although this is not always necessary. It is sensible to add some text that explains the plan, rather than leaving it as just a diagram (a bar chart usually known as a 'Gantt Chart').

The Business Case is the justification for the project. This has been produced in outline in Conception but in this phase it is developed further into a fully fledged Business Case that justifies the decision to go ahead with the Implementation phase. The Business Case is covered more fully in Chapter 2.

The Quality Plan is a strategy for ensuring that the required quality is delivered by the project. It will cover such aspects as which quality standards must be adhered to, how quality checking will be performed and who has the overall responsibility for quality. Chapter 7 explains quality in projects.

You can probably guess the function of Project Controls. These are ways in which the project is monitored and controlled throughout the life cycle. They enable the

Project Board to know that the project is on track, and they give the Project Manager confidence in the teams' progress. They are listed and explained in Chapter 10.

The Configuration Management Plan will describe how you will control all of the products produced by the project, and all of the different versions of these products. For example, any document may undergo various changes and each of the versions of the document needs to be identified and controlled. Chapter 8 covers this subject.

The Change Management Plan will describe the policy for managing change within the project. There can be many different changes in a project, and managing those changes using a controlled process is crucial to delivering a quality result. Uncontrolled change, also known as 'scope creep', can cause project chaos. Change management is detailed in Chapter 9.

The **'where'** is perhaps a little more tenuous, but you could apply this to the Project Plan as in, "In which stage is it done?", or maybe you have some geographical issues such as remote teams. In any case you do need to plan where the project teams are going to be housed and whether they have enough desks and equipment.

The set of roles within the project team that will be used in the project, and the names of those appointed to take those roles, are defined in the **Project Organisation Structure**. Structured Project Management relies heavily on people taking responsibility within the project and delivering what is required from them. Ideally a Project Organisation Structure should list the responsibilities of each role and each list should be accepted and signed off by the role-holder. Chapter 4 covers the subject of Project Organisation.

The Stakeholder Management Plan details the strategy for managing the stakeholders of the project. A stakeholder is anyone with an interest in the project, and this interest may be positive or negative. These people or organisations need to be managed carefully as they can have a potentially damaging effect on the project. Alternatively they can help to promote the project. Often the Stakeholder Management Plan is incorporated into the Communication Plan for the project, which lists the stakeholders and how they will be kept informed and involved throughout the project. This topic is covered in Chapter 5.

Throughout the rest of the project the PMP will be used as a basis for progress monitoring and control. That is why it covers so much about how the project will run, and also that is why it is signed off by the Project Board before the start of the next phase, Implementation. The approval of the PMP is another key activity that should confirm that the Project Board fully understands and accepts responsibility for ownership of the project. The Project Manager works under the direction of the Project Board and so follows the PMP, which can be considered as almost a 'contract' between the Project Manager and the Project Board.

One of the potentially difficult aspects of this phase is that it is lengthy, and therefore it costs a fair amount of money to carry it out. Commercial pressures can bear down on the Project Manager who is busy producing the PMP, but senior management may not be totally aware of exactly what the Project Manager is doing, and sometimes they ask questions as to why it is taking so long before the project actually produces technical results. This is why the Definition Phase Plan written in the Conception phase is so useful; it makes the Project Board fully aware of the activities the Project Manager will carry out in this phase, it lists the products that are contained within the PMP, and it will specify the estimated time and cost of the Definition phase. Also, as the Project Board has now approved the Definition Phase Plan at the end of the Conception phase, the members of the Board have had their expectations set and they have signed up to the amount of time and money spent during this phase.

Implementation

To understand this phase, it is useful to understand the meaning of the word 'product' in a project context. A product is the result of any activity; 'management' products help us to manage the project, whereas 'specialist' products are the project deliverables or elements that lead to deliverables, such as designs or specifications.

This will be the longest and costliest phase of the project, since this is where the technical specialists are producing and testing all of the specialist products. It is the phase where you, the Project Manager, follow the PMP to ensure that the project runs successfully and in the way approved by the Project Board. If there are elements of the PMP that are found to be in need of improvement, then it will be updated under formal change control. For example, stakeholders may complain about not being kept informed regularly enough, so the Communication Plan may need to be updated.

The Implementation phase is usually broken down further into stages, with each stage separated by a review and approval by the Project Board. Stages are a project control, and are discussed in Chapter 10.

The Implementation phase is complete when all of the project's products have been produced and successfully tested.

Handover and Closeout

This phase covers two main areas of the project: handover of the project's products into operational use, and administrative closure of the project. The principle of handover is to ensure that the products are delivered into a live environment successfully, and that they can be maintained properly from the first day of 'live' use. Closeout ensures that the project is reviewed and documentation is finalised. Customer Acceptance is one of the major outputs from this phase. Chapter 12, Handover and Closeout, discusses this phase in more detail.

Phase	Activities	Outputs
Conception	Justify the project. Decide whether to proceed into Definition.	Business Case. Definition Phase Plan.
Definition	Plan and define project. Decide whether to proceed into Implementation.	Project Management Plan.
Implementation	Develop project's products. Review viability of project at key points.	Developed and Tested. Products.
Handover and Closeout	Go live. Deliver products into operational support. Administrative closure.	Customer Acceptance. Operational products 'live'. Archived files.

Figure 1.6: Summary of the life cycle phases.

1.5 Project context

A project does not sit in isolation. It is surrounded by factors that will impact on it in many different ways. These factors are known as the project context. A useful way of remembering the elements of the project context is to remember the word 'PESTLE', a mnemonic which stands for:

- Political (government, industrial relations, political beliefs)
- Economic (interest rates, consumer spending, exchange rates)
- Sociological (people, demographics, attitudes and behaviours, lifestyle)
- Technical (scientific developments, suppliers, competitors)
- Legal (contracts, legislation)
- Environmental (climate, cultural differences, health and safety).

To illustrate the use of these factors, consider the following example project. You are managing the construction of a well in an African village. Using PESTLE, here are some of the factors that need to be considered in the project:

Political	Could we get funding from rich countries? Will a change of government impact on the project? Can we publicise the project to encourage more work of this type?
Economic	What is the cost of the project? How is it going to be funded? When will the funds arrive? Could we have a cash flow problem?
Sociological	Will there be any other impact on the villagers, apart from having clean water? Should we develop the area around the well into a meeting place?
Technical	What are the technical aspects of digging a well? Do we have that capability? Are there any advances in technology?
Legal	Do we have permission from the authorities to carry out the work? Are there any regulations we have to adhere to?
Environmental	What are the environmental implications of the construction? Will the project cause any pollution? How will we dispose of waste?

Figure 1.7: Example use of PESTLE.

Consideration of the external factors surrounding a project will assist with the proactive management of risks brought into the project by those factors. This needs to be done during the Conception phase of the project as it will probably have an impact on the Business Case. The project context should be reviewed during Definition as the project will have moved on and more factors may have come to light.

1.6 Summary

In this chapter you have learnt:

- ➢ The differences between projects and BAU
- ➢ The three targets for the Project Manager: delivering time, cost and quality

- ➢ What programmes and portfolios are, and why they are useful
- ➢ The phases of the project life cycle
- ➢ The definition and use of the project context.

The next chapter describes the purpose, contents and importance of the Business Case in the project. The Business Case is the basis for decision-making throughout the project.

1.7 Practical assignment

Read section A.1 of Appendix A—Background to the Case Study.

Document the context of the restaurant project.

1.8 Study

Answer the following multiple-choice questions. For answers see Appendix C.

1. Which is the best definition of a project?
   a) A weekly task.
   b) Minor improvements to an operational process.
   c) A set of tasks resulting in a significant change to the users.
   d) Carrying out a staff appraisal.
2. The statement which best defines the project life cycle is:
   a) Decide, Define, Develop, Deliver.
   b) Conception, Definition, Delivery, Handover and Closeout.
   c) Viability, Planning, Doing, Testing.
   d) Decide, Plan, Build, Test.
3. The elements of a project's context are:
   a) Political, Ergonomic, Social, Technical, Legal and Environmental.
   b) People, Economic, Scientific, Technical, Legislative and Ecological.
   c) Practical, Economic, Sociological, Technical, Legal and Environmental.
   d) Political, Economic, Sociological, Technical, Legal and Environmental.
4. A Project Manager's job is to:
   a) Motivate the teams to do the work.
   b) Deliver the project in accordance with the Project Management Plan.
   c) Ensure that the customer is satisfied, whatever the cost to the project.
   d) Deliver the benefits specified in the Business Case.
5. The relationship between time, cost and quality:
   a) Is always fixed for construction projects.
   b) Needs to be understood as it will be different for each project.
   c) Is specified by the Project Manager.
   d) Determines whether or not benefits will be realised.
6. The Project Management Plan:
   a) Forms the basis for progress monitoring throughout the project.
   b) Is written by the Project Board.
   c) Is approved by the Project Manager.
   d) Is approved by programme management.

The project manager's diary

I met Charlie for the first time today; he's a small, round man with a funny little 'Poirot' moustache and has a surprising energy and zest for life. The day I met him he'd already played golf and had two business meetings. We talked through his objectives and I was drawn in by his desire to launch the new restaurant and make it a big success.

I immediately agreed to take on the role of Project Manager. I told Charlie I would spend a couple of hours pulling some ideas together about how to move things forward and I pencilled in a meeting with him the following day.

In these situations I always remember the key principles: goals, objectives, scope, organisation, plan, risks etc…

The following day I met with Charlie and we spent a couple of hours in his office with a whiteboard and I sold to him the principles of structured methods and using a comprehensive Project Management Plan. He was sceptical at first but then I told him about the McTavish project that went wrong because they didn't use structured methods—McTavish finished three weeks early but made mistakes in building the wall, the whole thing had to be re-built and it ended up costing more and took longer. He asked me a lot of questions about the increased overheads of using a structured method; I explained the principle of 'right first time' which saves money in the long-term, and he seemed convinced by this. I don't think he'd come across pragmatic Project Management before.

I used PESTLE to brainstorm the project context with him, so that we could start to build a working relationship and get some common understanding. This helped us to identify some risks (which I noted down for inclusion in the Risk Log). Charlie was particularly worried when I pointed out the risk of not getting planning permission. We also found some key stakeholders (which I logged for consideration later on in Stakeholder Analysis). Whilst he was very aware of the need to ensure that the local residents enjoyed his Chicken Yaki Soba, he hadn't realised that local residents could be considered to be stakeholders in a more broad sense. For example, they might be concerned about the impact of lots of cars parking in the area, his neon sign on the street, or the smells from the kitchen. We identified a couple of actions for Charlie: talk to the local council to increase the chances that the Architect's plans will be granted planning permission on the first attempt, and do some market research on the local competition for the restaurant to assist with the Business Case.

2 Business Case: Ensure it is a viable project

This chapter explains the purpose and importance of a Business Case in a project. It describes the contents of a Business Case and how it is used throughout the project life cycle.

Have you ever:

- Worked on a project and wondered why the project was being undertaken?
- Been part way through a project and lost faith that the project was worth continuing with?
- Felt that the reasons for carrying out the project were not based on a sound foundation? (The answer to this question may depend on whether or not you have worked on a project from the side of the customer or the supplier; we'll return to this later.)

If you have answered 'yes' to any of these questions, then this chapter will help to clarify your causes for concern and how you might use a Business Case to resolve them.

In the last chapter we discussed the highly successful project to build the Millau Viaduct, which was delivered to specification within time and cost constraints. The original A75 motorway, which linked Clermont Ferrand and Beziers, passed through the town of Millau in the middle of the Tarn Valley. Motorists had to descend into the valley through a steep road and cross the town of Millau, to reach the other end of the valley. The roads were generally crowded and the situation worsened in the summer months when motorists took close to three hours to cross the valley. After an initial period of increased traffic congestion caused by sightseers, the viaduct has delivered its predicted benefits by providing a route across the Tarn Valley and reducing congestion in the area. The 24 km (15 mile) journey up and down the Tarn Valley, which had earlier taken three hours, has been reduced to less than 20 minutes.

Consider the project to build the Channel Tunnel, which was completed in 1994. It is the second-longest rail tunnel in the world, and the longest undersea tunnel in the world. At completion, the whole project had cost around £10 billion, which was an overspend of about 80%. Since the project completion, the tunnel has been operating at a large loss; £1.33 billion in 2003 and £570 million in 2004. Shares of the stock that funded the project dropped by 90% of their value between 1989 and 1998. The reasons for this have been given as high interest payments because of the debt and the volume of passenger and freight traffic being much less than the forecasts—only 38% and 24%, respectively.

Surely some serious questions about the Business Case for the Channel Tunnel have to be asked. As Eurotunnel is a privately owned company, the justification for the project was to make a profit. Was the project researched properly? 38% or 24% of forecast usage is extremely low. Was the Business Case used correctly during the Channel Tunnel project?

2.1 Purpose of a Business Case

The Business Case has a number of objectives:

- Project validation; to carry out an internal check to ensure that the project is worth doing, i.e., the benefits outweigh the costs
- Responding to events; if something changes during the project, the Business Case enables repetition of the internal check
- Internal communications; to ensure that all of the stakeholders are aware of the benefits.

The Business Case is the key document within the Project Management Plan (PMP). At any time during the project we can refer to the Business Case to see whether the project is still justified, and to check that the relevant elements of the business environment have not changed significantly.

The ultimate success of a project is measured by the realisation of the benefits, so the benefits as described in the Business Case drive the project. All decisions about the project should be made by considering the expected benefits.

It is important to note that a Business Case is written to justify the amount to be invested in the project, so it is written from the perspective of the customer (who is funding the project), rather than the supplier (who is supplying work to the project). In other words, the Business Case says, "What return can we expect on our investment?" or "How much is it going to cost us to achieve these benefits for our business?"

Who is involved?

The Project Sponsor owns the Business Case and therefore will usually produce it. However, it is possible that the Project Sponsor will oversee the development of the Business Case by the Project Manager. In many environments the Project Manager does all of the 'leg work' and the Project Sponsor directs and approves the Project Manager's work. But even if the Project Sponsor delegates this work to the Project Manager, the Project Sponsor still owns the project and therefore owns the Business Case as well.

For more details on the responsibilities of each role in the project, see Chapter 4: Project Organisation.

2.2 Business Case contents

Different organisations will write Business Cases in different ways. But these are the items that should always be included as a minimum:

Reasons: These are the reasons why we are considering carrying out the project. This tends to be a description of the current situation. For example, if the proposed project is to move house, the reason might be that we are not happy with the current area in which we live. If the suggested project is to produce a new computer system, the reasons for the project might include the fact that the old system is costing the organisation too much to maintain.

Options: these are the options that have been considered, which may solve the current problem or situation. There may only be one option, but normally there will be a few. Including 'Options' as an item ensures that all options are considered. One of the options that should always be considered is 'do nothing'; sometimes organisations can get carried away with the thought of a bright, shiny new product, whereas actually the most cost-effective option may be to stick with what they already have.

> "The best way to have a good idea is to have lots of ideas."
> Linus Pauling (American theoretical physical chemist)

Benefits: these are the positive outcomes that the project is expected to bring into the organisation. In commercial environments, benefits are usually financial, such as increased revenue or cost savings. Even benefits that at first sight seem to be non-financial can often be translated into financial ones. For example 'improved staff morale' will translate into 'reduced staff turnover' and then into 'reduction in recruitment and training costs'.

Benefits are best stated in measurable terms. If the benefits are financial, this is fairly easily done. If they are intangible, for instance 'improved educational facilities', then some form of measurement needs to be contrived, if at all possible. You could measure 'improved educational facilities' by surveying a large number of people and specifying a target of 80% of those questioned agreeing that the educational facilities have been improved. Quantification of intangible factors is often hard to do and controversial; there are inevitably many different opinions as to the true value of something that is hard to measure.

Most projects will have a mixture of tangible (usually financial) benefits and intangible benefits.

Sometimes the benefits of carrying out a project relate more to the reasons that we cannot avoid doing it. For instance, if we do not update the accounting system to take account of the new VAT laws, we will be in violation of the law.

Cost and time: these are simple notes of the estimated cost and time of the project, so that the benefits can be compared against the cost, and the time taken to develop the project can be taken into account against the benefits. If there is a cost impact on the rest of the customer organisation, then this should be included.

Risks: these are the major risks against achieving the benefits. Detailing them enables the risks to be compared against the benefits. It may be that our assessment of the risks of the project means that the risks outweigh the potential benefits, so we may not continue with the project. It is often the case that a high benefit project is high risk, and equally a low risk project often achieves relatively low benefits (compare the race to put a man on the moon versus putting up some shelves in your study).

Cost-Benefit analysis: this is the mathematical comparison of the negative costs against the positive benefits. This is relevant where the benefits of a project are financial and so can be compared against the costs. There are a few methods of undertaking this, but the simplest is the Payback method. The Payback method lists the costs in each year, the financial benefits in each year, then calculates the cash flow for each year and works out the cumulative cash flow through the next five years of operation.

For example, an IT project to replace a legacy system has a development cost of £100K and an operational cost of £20K each year after that. The legacy system was expensive to maintain and savings of £50K per year will be made once the new system is in place. The Payback calculations would be as follows:

Year	0	1	2	3	4	5
Costs	(100)	(20)	(20)	(20)	(20)	(20)
Benefits	0	50	50	50	50	50
Cash flow	(100)	30	30	30	30	30
Cumulative Cash flow	(100)	(70)	(40)	(10)	(20)	50

Figure 2.1: Example Payback calculation.

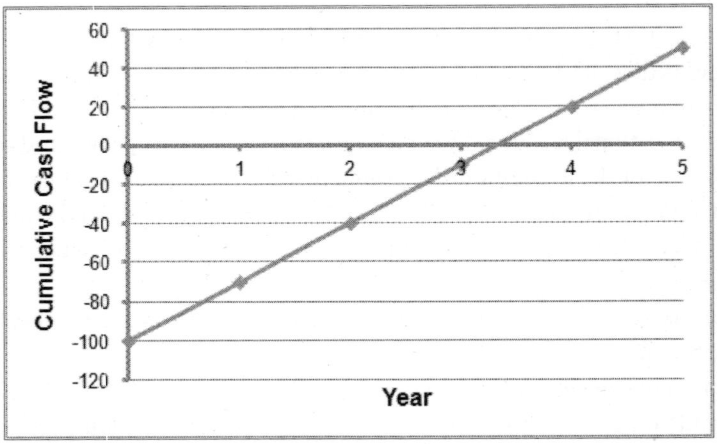

Figure 2.2: Example Payback graph.

Typically this method uses year 0 as the starting point, when the development work is undertaken, and then covers the next five years' use of the new products. Costs are shown in brackets to denote a negative value.

Cash flow is the simple subtraction of costs from benefits, in each year. (So in year 1, cash flow is 50–20 = 30.)

Cumulative cash flow is the sum of the cash flow figures totalled up as you go, so that you can see the position after each year, similar to the balance in a bank account. So cumulative cash flow in year 1 is calculated by taking the cumulative cash flow in year 0 and adding the cash flow in year 1, i.e., (100) + 30 = (70).

This calculation shows that Payback, that is when we will break even, occurs in year 3, as this is when the cumulative cash flow figures become positive, i.e., the project is 'in the black' in its bank account.

This is a very simple method of cost-benefit analysis. There are other methods which involve taking into account the decreasing value of money over time. For details of these methods, see the further reading references in Appendix D.

Conclusion

This is a note to say whether or not the project is justified, on the basis of the preceding contents.

> "In any moment of decision the best thing you can do is the right thing, the next best thing is the wrong thing, and the worst thing you can do is nothing."
> Attributed to Theodore Roosevelt

2.3 Life cycle of the Business Case

We can now relate the development and monitoring of the Business Case to the project life cycle.

During Conception, an outline Business Case is put together in order to justify continuing with the project into the Definition phase. Details of what is proposed may be fairly sketchy at this time, but as a minimum it should give an idea of overall cost and time and major risks against predicted business benefits.

During Definition, a complete Business Case is produced which fully justifies the project.

During Implementation, the Business Case must be kept up-to-date so that at any point we can check it against any changes requested or major Issues that arise. It will also be checked each time the project is reviewed, to ensure that the project remains justified. If the project is found to be no longer worthwhile, because the Business Case does not 'stand up', then it should be closed. Bear in mind that there may be costs involved with closing the project, so these should be taken into account.

During Handover and Closeout, an evaluation of the project will take place. The latest version of the Business Case should be compared against the actual results of the project. However, it is nearly always the case that it is too early to measure achievement of the business benefits; we need to actually use the project's products in order to measure these. For example, if we have implemented a new website with the predicted benefit of generating more sales, when we handover the project and the website goes live, we have no idea yet as to whether more sales will be achieved. Measurement of the achievement of the business benefits will take place some time after the end of the project, maybe years afterwards. This is known as the Benefits Realisation Review. If the Business Case specifies that sales will be increased each year and that after five years they will be up by 100%, then we need to wait five years in order to be sure that the 100% increase has been achieved.

This means that the project should be designed with long-term reporting capabilities built in. In the future when the customer is considering whether to embark on a similar project, the Business Case analysis may well begin with the question, "What were the benefits last time?" The profitability of a restaurant will be easily visible from the accounts, but the benefits of a software project embedded in (say) a vehicle production system, will be much harder to see. The software should be designed to produce monthly performance reports to ensure that the benefits are visible.

Phase	Business Case Development and Monitoring
Conception	Outline Business Case developed
Definition	Full Business Case in PMP
Implementation	Business Case checked and updated at each review point Impact of changes checked against Business Case
Handover and Closeout	Final outcome of project compared with latest version of Business Case
After the end of the project	Achievement of the business benefits measured in a Benefits Realisation Review

Figure 2.3: Development and use of the Business Case.

2.4 Supplier's Business Case

The Business Case for the project is written from the perspective of the organisation paying for the project, so it is really the customer's Business Case. If you normally work on the supplier side of the customer- supplier relationship, you may not even see your customer's Business Case as this may be confidential. If you are an internal supplier, for example you work in the IT department of a large organisation, then it is possible that you will see the Business Case. If you are an external supplier then it is less likely that you will see the customer's Business Case, although sometimes external suppliers will help the customer to develop the Business Case.

The supplier also has a reason for being involved in a project. If the supplier is an external organisation, then the supplier's Business Case will usually be fairly simple—to make a profit from this contract. Suppliers do not normally formally document this as a Business Case, but will usually have a breakdown of their costs which will show the margin between the total cost and the price they will charge the customer.

2.5 Summary

In this chapter you have learnt:

- How the Business Case drives the project
- That the Business Case should be updated throughout the project
- What are the essential elements of the Business Case
- That measurement of the business benefits can only be made some time after the end of the project.

The next chapter shows you how to plan a project, to ensure that before the project starts you have a realistic set of activities and costs set against the allowed timescale.

2.6 Practical assignment

Read section A.2 of Appendix A—Information for the Business Case.

Write a Business Case for the restaurant project.

2.7 Study

Answer the following multiple-choice questions. For answers see Appendix C.

1. Which role in the project owns the Business Case?
   a) Project Manager.
   b) Project Sponsor.
   c) Accountant.
   d) Everyone.
2. When can measurement of achievement of the benefits be performed?
   a) Every time the Business Case is reviewed.
   b) On the first day of live use of the project's deliverables.
   c) When the project is evaluated during Closeout.
   d) After a period of live use of the project's deliverables.
3. Which of the following statements is true?
   a) Every project should have a Business Case.
   b) A Business Case is not required for small projects.
   c) A Business Case is not required if a project is part of a programme.
   d) A Business Case is not required if the Project Sponsor has decided the project will go ahead anyway.
4. Why should a Business Case include major project risks?
   a) To inform the Sponsor about the key risks.
   b) These will be reviewed during handover.
   c) This allows the risks to be weighed up against the benefits.
   d) To inform the supplier about the key risks.

The project manager's diary

After three days' hard work, I'd written the Business Case and planned the Definition Phase, so I reckoned I'd completed the Conception phase and it was time for Charlie to review the project viability. I tried to contact Charlie to arrange the next meeting but he was difficult to get hold of, and apparently had his mobile switched off whilst playing golf. Eventually we agreed a meeting for the Friday afternoon at 4pm (!). This caused me to start my own private risk log, which no-one else will see, and note down the risk that Charlie does not own the project properly. Mind you, that's fairly normal, just like all the Sponsors I've worked for.

Anyway we had the meeting and he was very pleased with the profit figures of £13K per month in the Business Case, but the sticking point was the Definition Phase Plan. He wouldn't accept that to write a PMP would take me so long, and we ended up going over some of the same ground again from the first meeting. I tried to illustrate why it was so important to agree all of the management processes to be used on the project before the technical work started. I ended up having to tell him about getting the foundations of the project right from the start, before any development work is done, so that the project didn't end up with 'wobbly walls'. I think this analogy helped him. Finally he approved my proposed cost and time, gave me 5% tolerance on each and I booked the next meeting (to approve the PMP) in his diary, making sure he had no golf that day!

As the Business Case was approved, I added the risks mentioned in it into the Risk Log to ensure I didn't forget them for the Risk Brainstorming session.

Thank goodness that phase is done with; now I can get on with the real work of putting together the PMP.

3 Project planning: Create a workable plan

This chapter takes you through the steps of creating a Project Plan. This will provide an essential picture of the project's activities set against a timescale. It will provide an estimate of the project's duration and will show the planned start and finish dates for each activity. This enables the Project Manager to agree a sufficient budget and realistic timescale with the Project Sponsor.

Throughout the project, the Project Plan will be used as a baseline against which progress will be compared, giving the Project Manager early warning of delays or other problems which could reduce the chances of project success.

The Project Plan is a key element of the Project Management Plan (PMP). It documents the activities, resource requirements and schedules for the project. It should provide confidence that the project objectives are achievable within the constraints of time and cost. It needs to be kept up-to-date throughout the project to reflect:

Progress already made, and any changes to:

- The forecast end date.
- The forecast project cost.
- Functionality and scope.
- Resource requirements.

"The plan is nothing; the planning is everything."
Dwight Eisenhower

Project planning comprises many steps, each building on the previous one. In order to explain these steps effectively we will use the example of a really simple project to decorate a room, to highlight the essential stages that occur in planning any project, however large. This project includes laying a new carpet, painting the walls, ceiling and woodwork, and installing some new furniture.

3.1 Step 1: Work Breakdown Structure (WBS)

The first step is to break down the work involved in the project on a (WBS):

The WBS shows the scope of the project, that is to say, the total work content of the project. Importantly, by omission, it also shows the exclusions from the scope, for example, in this project it is clear that we are not going to do any wallpapering. This picture of the project is a useful visual aid and can easily be used in brainstorming sessions with key project stakeholders such as customers, technical teams and users. There is no time implied in the WBS; although it feels sensible to put 'buy paint' before 'paint walls and ceiling', in the strictest sense all that the WBS does is to identify the tasks in the project and put them into sensible groups. At this point we are not concerned with dependencies between these tasks. For example, we will obviously delay installing the furniture until the carpet has been laid, but this analysis comes later on in this process.

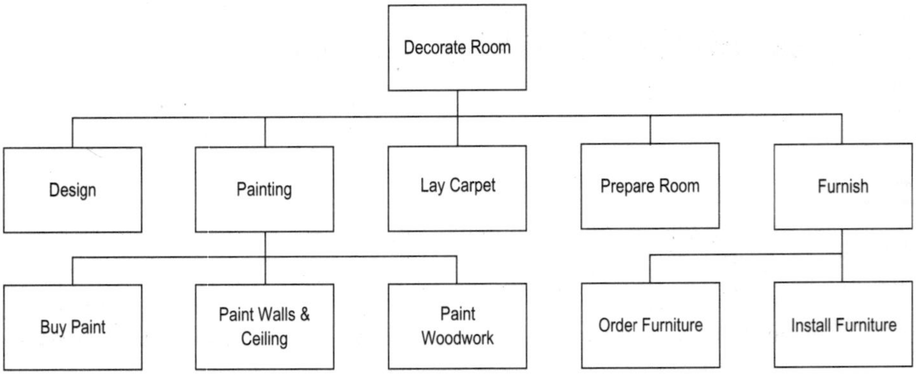

Figure 3.1: Work Breakdown Structure.

It is usual to add Task Reference numbers to the WBS so that each task is uniquely identified. So the WBS would now look like this:

The task references show the parent–child relationships between the tasks. There are different numbering conventions you can use, but one of the industry standard conventions is one based on hierarchical references, i.e., where the number of digits in the reference

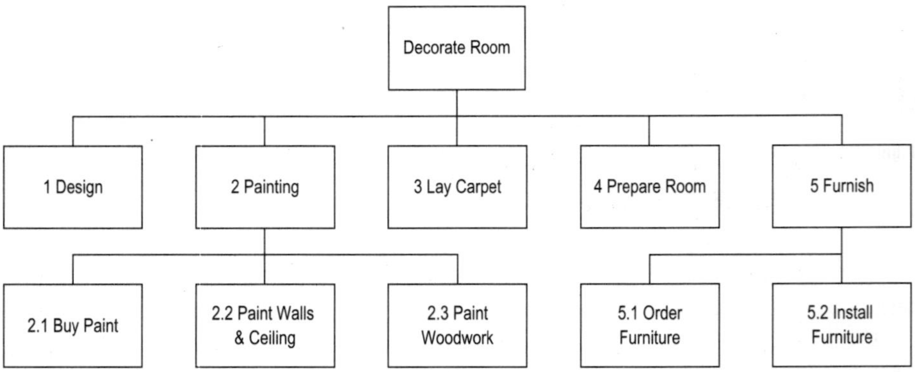

Figure 3.2: Work Breakdown Structure with task references.

number reflects the task's position in the hierarchy; if we divided 'Install Furniture' into two tasks such as 'Install Table' and 'Install Chairs' then they would be numbered '5.2.1' and '5.2.2' respectively. These hierarchical references tend to be used when entering the plan details into a software planning tool such as Microsoft Project.

Once you are happy with the WBS, it is important to identify the lowest level (or simple) tasks. These are the tasks that your team will need to undertake and are not broken down any further in the WBS, as they can be estimated quite accurately. We will assign letters to these tasks as follows:

Task Id	Task Description
A	Design Layout
B	Prepare Room
C	Buy paint
D	Paint walls and ceiling
E	Paint woodwork
F	Lay carpet
G	Order furniture
H	Install furniture

Figure 3.3: Tasks to decorate a room.

So we now have two sets of identifiers: Task References and Task Ids. We will use the Task Ids when we are interested in only the simple tasks, for example, when working out task dependencies. We will use the Task References when we want to show the task hierarchy, for example, in the overall project plan.

3.2 Step 2: Cost Breakdown Structure

The purpose of a Cost Breakdown Structure (CBS) is to provide a pictorial view of the costs in the project. The WBS is used as a basis, and each task is labelled with the estimated cost. So for the decorated room the CBS may look like this:

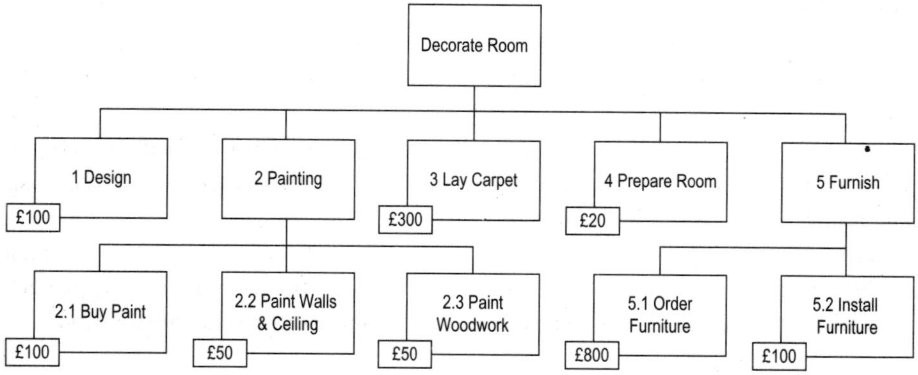

Figure 3.4: Cost Breakdown Structure.

The costs shown above are the combined costs of labour and materials for each task. It may be useful to show labour and materials costs separately.

The total cost of the tasks in the project can now be summarised. So the total cost of Painting is £200 and the total cost of Furnishing is £900. The total cost of project tasks is therefore £1,520. This shows where the main cost of the project lies, so if the project is considered too expensive then it is easy to see where the largest savings can be made.

The total cost of the project will be greater than £1,520. We need to add in the cost of Project Management, risk mitigation, and possibly allow for the cost of changes. These are covered in later chapters. The control of costs through the project is an important factor in meeting project success criteria, and is usually managed using a spreadsheet known as a Cost Account. This is covered in Chapter 10: Project Controls.

3.3 Step 3: Organisational Breakdown Structure

The Organisational Breakdown Structure (OBS) shows the resources required by the project. It is drawn using a hierarchy to denote the reporting lines. It can be based on the WBS, if the WBS groups the tasks in the project according to the skills required. So for the decorated room, the OBS might look like this:

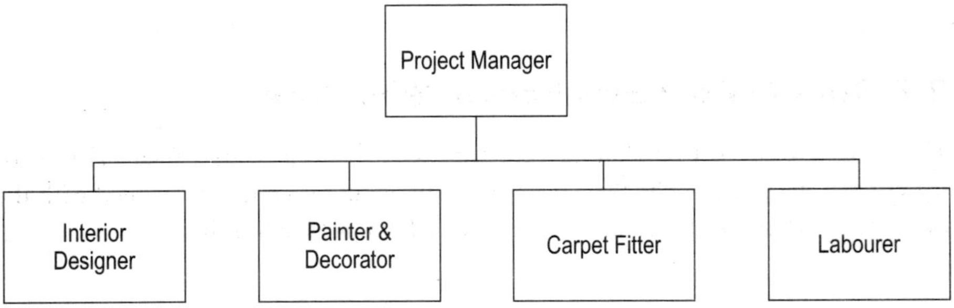

Figure 3.5: Organisational Breakdown Structure.

The Labourer will be responsible for preparing the room and installing the furniture.

The OBS for this example is very simple. For larger projects there will probably be a role of 'team leader' who would manage a team of resources carrying out the tasks, and report to the Project Manager.

The OBS does not show all of the lines of communication during the project; most of these resources will need to talk to each other about the tasks during the project. The following section shows a technique used to show these task consultations.

3.4 Step 4: Responsibility Assignment Matrix

The Responsibility Assignment Matrix (RAM) uses both the WBS and the OBS to assign tasks to resources. A key is used to denote the way in which the resource is involved in the task. So in the case of the decorated room, a RAM could be as follows:

Task Id.	Description	Project Manager	Interior Designer	Painter	Carpet Fitter	Labourer
A	Design Layout	A	R			
C	Buy Paint	A	C	R		
D	Paint Walls and Ceiling	A		R		
E	Paint Woodwork	A		R	I	
F	Lay Carpet	A			R	I
B	Prepare Room	A				R
G	Order Furniture	A	R			C
H	Install Furniture	A				R

Figure 3.6: Responsibility Assignment Matrix.

The meanings of the codes are:

A—The role is Accountable for this task

R—The role is Responsible for carrying out this task

C—The role will be consulted when this task is carried out

I—The role will be informed of the outcome of this task.

Only the simple tasks are used in this table. In this example, the Project Manager is accountable for all tasks, but in a larger project with team leaders in the OBS it may be that the team leaders are made accountable for the tasks carried out by their team members.

The RAM shows the Project Manager that all tasks have at least one person responsible for them, so no tasks have been forgotten. It also shows the workload (in terms of tasks) for each resource, so that any potential overload on a resource can be avoided. It gives each resource a view of how their work fits into the project.

3.5 Step 5: Network diagrams

Network diagrams are a way of showing the project tasks in a diagrammatic form, this helps in the calculation of the project duration and identification of some project risks.

The first step in producing a network diagram is to consider the dependencies between the tasks. The simplest form of dependency is called a 'finish-to-start' dependency, where the next task cannot start until the previous one has finished.

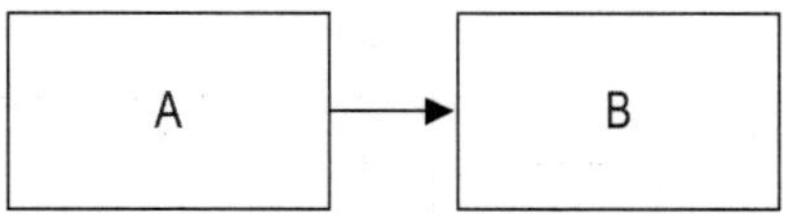

Figure 3.7: Finish-to-start dependency.

The diagramming convention uses rectangular boxes for the tasks and arrows for the dependencies. So if Task B is dependent on Task A, the diagram will look like this:

Now using the example of the decorated room, we can work out the dependencies for the tasks as follows:

Task Id.	Task Description	Dependency
A	Design Layout	
B	Prepare Room	A
C	Buy paint	A
D	Paint walls and ceiling	B and C
E	Paint woodwork	D
F	Lay carpet	E
G	Order furniture	A
H	Install furniture	F and G

Figure 3.8: Task dependencies for decorating a room.

However, it is not strictly true to say that 'install furniture' is dependent only on 'lay carpet' and 'order furniture'. Once we've ordered the furniture, it may take weeks to be delivered. One way to overcome this problem with the dependencies is to add in a 'dummy' task called 'await furniture delivery'. So now the list of dependencies looks like this:

Task Id	Task Description	Dependency
A	Design Layout	
B	Prepare Room	A
C	Buy paint	A
D	Paint walls and ceiling	B and C
E	Paint woodwork	D
F	Lay carpet	E
G	Order furniture	A
H	Await furniture delivery	G
I	Install furniture	E and H

Figure 3.9: Updated tasks for decorating a room.

And the dependency network is as follows:

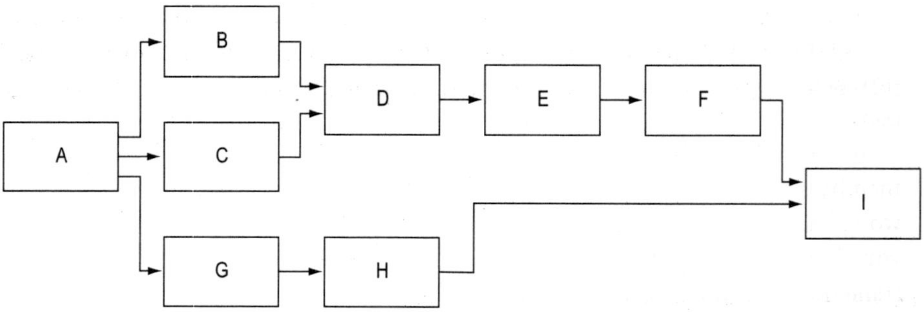

Figure 3.10: Network diagram for decorating a room.

This is also known as a 'precedence network' or 'PERT chart'.

This example has been based on a very small project. For large projects, the network diagram may become very large and complicated. The Project Manager needs to consider the level of tasks that are used in the network; if the lowest possible level of task is used in the network for a very large project, updating the PERT network can become a large overhead and may not be done. It may be better to use summary tasks to keep the network to a reasonable size.

3.6 Step 6: Estimating

Estimating is predicting a quantitative value for something. At this point in the Planning process we need to estimate the duration of each activity in the network. There is a difference between the effort needed to complete a task and the duration that the task will take. This is because more than one resource will often work on a task together. So for example, two resources may each spend 4 days on a task. The duration of the task is 4 days but the effort is 8 days.

Even if you have only one resource working on a task, there is a difference between effort and duration. This is because, during the working day, people working on your project are not working 100% on the project task. In the course of a year, people will take annual leave, attend training courses and possibly take sick leave, plus there are usually company meetings to attend. A simple breakdown of the 365 days in a year gives an idea of the percentage of the working year that will be spent on productive project work:

Number of days in a year:		**365**
Weekend days	104	
Bank holidays	8	
Number of working days per year:		**253**
Annual leave	25	
Training courses	10	
Sick leave	5	
Company meetings	2	
Number of days worked per year:		**211**

Figure 3.11: Table of working days per year.

This means that the percentage of available time that people are actually performing productive work is 211/253 = 83%. Most companies have a standard percentage that is consistently applied to project planning; typically this ranges from 80–90%.

If you are planning a long-term project, then you may not know when your team members are planning to take holidays or going on training courses, and you certainly won't know when they are going to be ill! So you can use this percentage to ensure that your long-term project plan allows for these things. For example, if your company standard percentage is 80%, then a task estimated to take 4 weeks should be planned in at 5 weeks' duration.

The duration figures are the ones that can be applied to the precedence network to provide an indication of the overall duration of the project. This is covered in the next step.

As you progress through the project, the type of estimating carried out varies and you will find that the accuracy of the estimating improves:

- In the Conception phase of the project, you may only be able to arrive at a "ball-park" estimate, known as **Subjective** estimating. As the name suggests, this has a very low level of accuracy. For example, we could say that to decorate the room will take between two and four weeks.
- A little later on, in the Definition phase, you may be in a position to compare the project with previous projects. By asking questions such as, "Is this project smaller or larger?", "Is this project more or less complex?" and "Are we using similar methods or different ones?", you can assess what adjustments you need to make to the effort figures for the previous projects to arrive at an estimate for this project. This is called **Comparative** estimating.
- Later in the project, when some work has been done in the Implementation phase, you can use historical data to arrive at more accurate estimates. For example, once we have painted one wall, we know how long it actually took and this information can be used with a parameter to create an estimate. In this example, the parameter would be the number of walls requiring painting. This is called **Parametric**

estimating. This is the most accurate form of estimating. As already mentioned, the accuracy of estimates improves as the project progresses, and this feature of estimating is sometimes known as the 'estimating funnel'—as time progresses, estimating converges on accuracy.

- **Bottom-up** estimating takes the low-level tasks from a WBS and estimates each task individually. The figures are then totalled upwards in the structure to provide an estimate for the whole project. An example of this method has already been seen in the CBS earlier in this chapter.

3.7 Step 7: Critical Path Analysis

Once the duration of each task in the precedence network has been estimated, these figures are used to calculate the duration of the project using the following technique.

Critical Path Analysis uses simple addition and subtraction on the 'nodes' of the precedence network. The node is the rectangular box in which so far we have simply added the task identifier. Each node has a set of information about the task, as follows:

<table>
<tr><td>Earliest Start Time</td><td>Duration</td><td>Earliest Finish Time</td></tr>
<tr><td colspan="3">Task Identifier</td></tr>
<tr><td>Latest Start Time</td><td>Total Float</td><td>Latest Finish Time</td></tr>
</table>

Figure 3.12: Information in a node.

The meanings of each cell are:

- The Earliest Start Time is the soonest that the task can start
- The Duration is the length of time that the task will take
- The Earliest Finish Time is the soonest that the task can finish
- The Latest Start Time is the latest that the task can start
- The Latest Finish Time is the latest that the task can finish
- The Total Float is the amount of delay that could occur on the task before the project end date is delayed as a consequence. For example, if the Total Float is zero then the task cannot be delayed without affecting the whole project.

Forward pass

Once the duration of each task has been entered into each node, a forward pass is carried out on the network. This completes the top row of each node, starting with the first task and ending with the last one. The first step is to fill in the Earliest Start of the first task as day 0. For each task, the Duration is added to the Earliest Start to obtain the Earliest Finish. The Earliest Finish of a task becomes the Earliest Start of any dependent tasks.

For example, using generic tasks A, B, C and D, if the network looked like this:

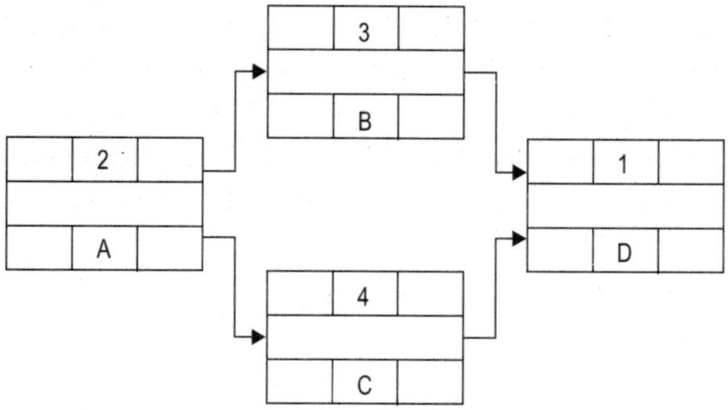

Figure 3.13: Network with duration figures.

Then performing the Forward Pass would result in:

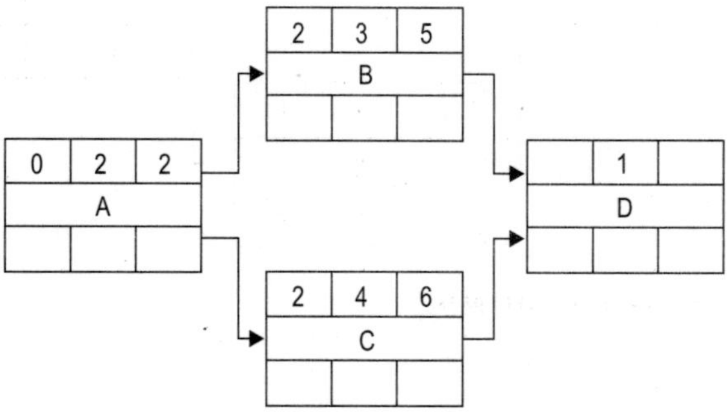

Figure 3.14: Network with partial forward pass.

For the Earliest Start of task D, there is a choice; should it be the Earliest Finish of B or C that is used? As we are looking for the earliest possible start of D, it must be the higher of the two figures that is used, as D is dependent on the completion of both B and C. So the figure 6 from task C is used and the network now looks like this:

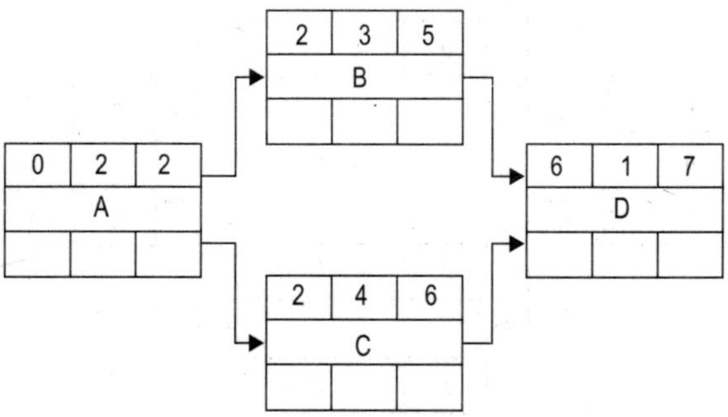

Figure 3.15: Network with complete forward pass.

The shortest possible time in which this project can be completed is 7 days.

Backward pass

The Earliest Finish of Task D is then used as the Latest Finish for task D and we can complete the network working backwards. For each task, the Duration is subtracted from the Latest Finish to obtain the Latest Start. The Latest Finish of a task becomes the Latest Start of any dependent tasks. The Total Float is the difference between the Latest Finish and Earliest Finish (or Latest Start and Earliest Start, as this will be the same value).

Now the network is as follows:

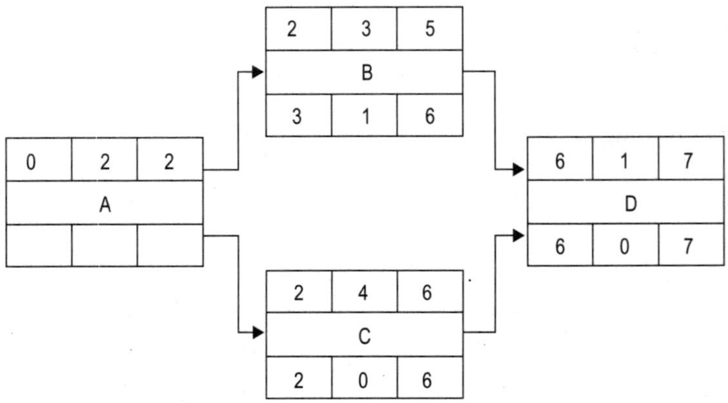

Figure 3.16: Network with partial backward pass.

For the Latest Finish of task A, there is a choice; should it be the Latest Start of B or C that is used? As we are looking for the latest possible finish of A, it must be the lower of the two figures that is used, as both B and C are dependent on the completion of A. So the figure 2 from task C is used and the network now looks like this:

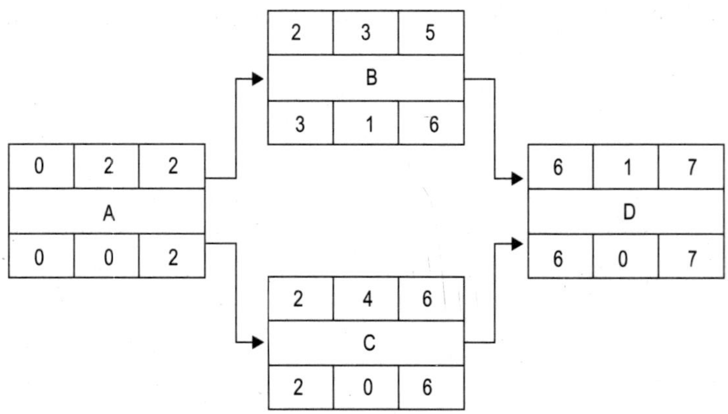

Figure 3.17: Network with complete backward pass.

To summarise the steps of network analysis:

1. Enter the duration of each task
2. Start with a 0 for the Earliest Start of the first task
3. Perform the Forward Pass:
    - For each task, Earliest Finish = Earliest Start + Duration
    - Earliest Start of next task = Earliest Finish of preceding task
    - When there is a choice for Earliest Start, take the highest value
4. For the last task, the Latest Finish = Earliest Finish
5. Perform the Backward Pass:
    - For each task, Latest Start = Latest Finish-Duration
    - Latest Finish of preceding task = Latest Start of next task
    - When there is a choice for Latest Finish, take the lowest value.
6. For each task, Total Float = Latest Start-Earliest Start.

The Critical Path of the network is the longest path through the network. In this simple example it is easy to see from the first diagram that the longest path is A, C and D. A more complex network requires the network to be analysed and the path with zero total float in each node is the Critical Path. The critical path is therefore the path through the network that comprises tasks which, if any of them are delayed, will delay the end date of the project. Therefore this shows the Project Manager the more risky tasks in the project.

There is another type of float: Free Float. This is defined as the amount a task can be delayed without affecting the next activity in the network. Free Float is always less than or equal to Total Float, so if a task has zero Total Float then Free Float will also be zero. Free Float occurs only when one task in the network is dependent on two or more tasks.

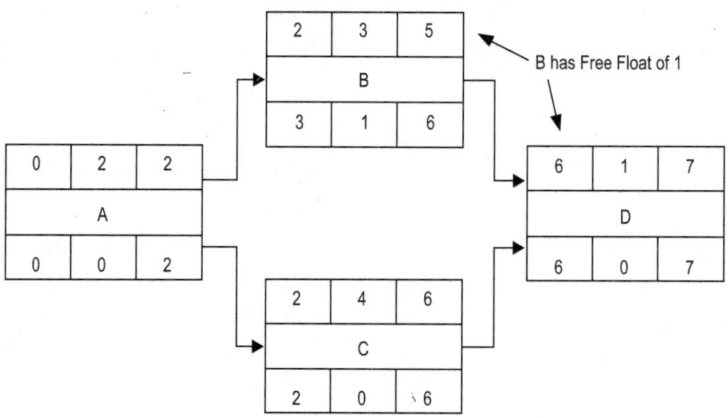

Figure 3.18: Network with free float.

Task B has a Free Float of 1 because the Earliest Start of Task D is caused by the Earliest Finish of Task C. So if Task C is painting the walls of a room, Task B is painting the ceiling and Task C is laying the carpet, then Task B can be delayed one day if necessary.

Returning to the example of the project to decorate a room, based on the task durations in the table below, the network analysis produces the network as in Figure 3.20:

Task Id	Task Description	Duration
A	Design Layout	3
B	Prepare Room	3
C	Buy paint	1
D	Paint walls and ceiling	2
E	Paint woodwork	2
F	Lay carpet	1
G	Order furniture	1
H	Await furniture delivery	10
I	Install furniture	1

Figure 3.19: Task durations for decorating a room.

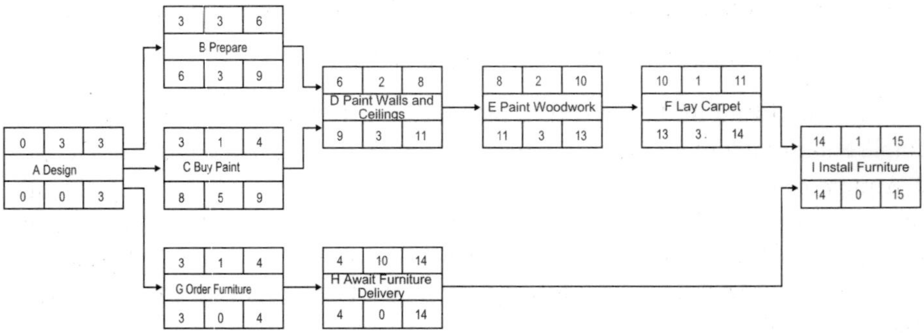

Figure 3.20: Network for decorating a room.

One of the main benefits of a network diagram is that when project events don't go according to plan, you can easily see the impact of the problem on the project. For example, in Figure 3.20, if we cannot buy the paint in one day, as perhaps it has to be ordered and will take a week, this will delay the whole project. The network can be used to show delays on the project; take a copy of the baseline version and then the current version can be used as a comparison.

Whilst the PERT network can be a useful visual guide, over-reliance on it can be a potential problem for the Project Manager. The PERT network used on the project to build Concorde consisted of approximately 800 tasks. This made it very complicated and slow to respond to changes. It can be that checking project progress against milestones is more effective than attempting to maintain a huge, unwieldy chart. One person on the Concorde project was quoted as saying, "People looked at the charts and not out of the window at what was happening in the factory." The network is more useful to identify bottlenecks in the plan and the critical path, and should be kept to a more sensible, smaller number of tasks or used to represent a sub-project.

3.8 Step 8: Gantt chart

This information can now be entered into a Gantt Chart. A Gantt chart, also known as a bar chart or schedule, shows the activities of a project mapped against a timescale.

This provides a useful map of the project. At this point you could enter the activities, dependencies and durations into a software planning tool such as Microsoft Project which will generate the Gantt chart automatically. In a simple example such as this, it is probably easier to use a simple tool such as Microsoft Excel to produce the Gantt chart:

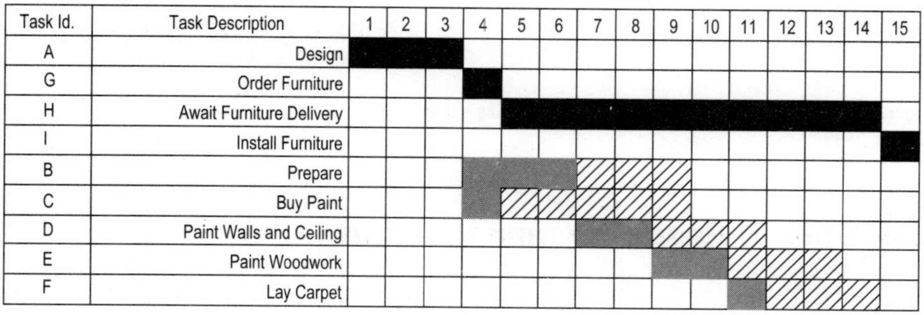

Figure 3.21: Microsoft excel Gantt chart for decorating a room.

The critical path is drawn on the chart first, and is shown here in bold. Then each non-critical activity is added using the earliest finish time and duration. The total float of each non-critical activity is shown in the hatched boxes.

So immediately it is clear that the activity which has the greatest effect on the project duration is the waiting time for delivery of the furniture. If the Project Manager wants to reduce the project duration, there will not be much to be gained from reducing the duration of the non-critical activities. If the furniture could be delivered on the day after ordering it, then the critical path would be very different:

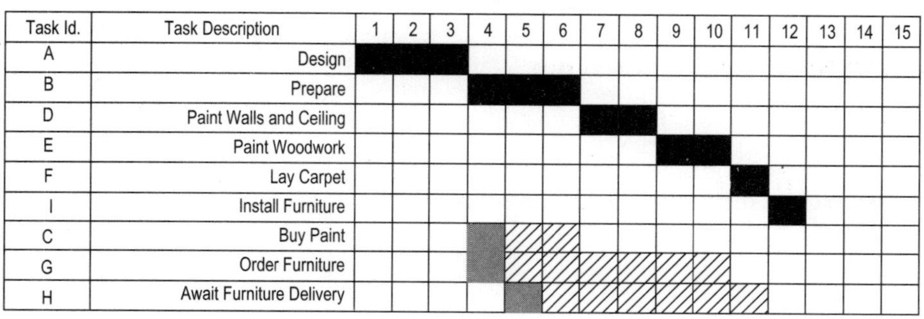

Figure 3.22: Adjusted Microsoft Excel Gantt chart for decorating a room.

This Gantt chart shows only the simple tasks from the WBS. It is common practice for the summary tasks to be included as well. Figure 3.23 below shows the previous example again but this time the diagram is generated by Microsoft Project. The hierarchical task references from the WBS are now shown in the Task Name column.

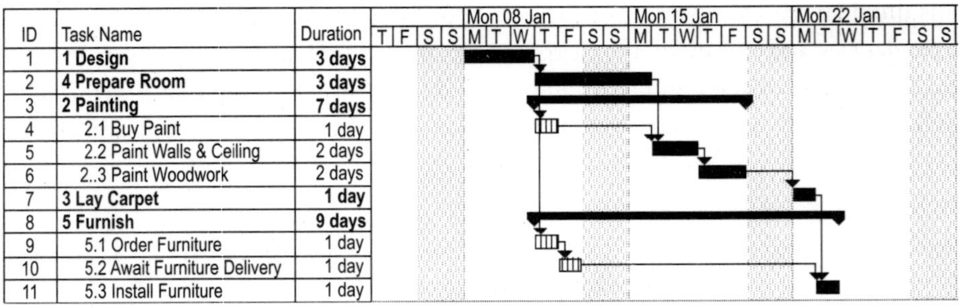

Figure 3.23: Microsoft project Gantt chart for decorating a room.

3.9 Step 9: Resource management

To complete the schedule, we need to make sure that we have enough resources available to carry out the tasks each day of the plan. To do this, a resource histogram is drawn. A histogram is a frequency chart, in this case a chart of the number of resources used per day in the project.

Using the number of resources per task as follows:

Task Id	Task Description	No. of Resources
A	Design Layout	2
B	Prepare Room	2
C	Buy paint	1
D	Paint walls and ceiling	2
E	Paint woodwork	1
F	Lay carpet	2
G	Order furniture	1
H	Await furniture delivery	0
I	Install furniture	1

Figure 3.24: Task resources for decorating a room.

The resource histogram will look like this:

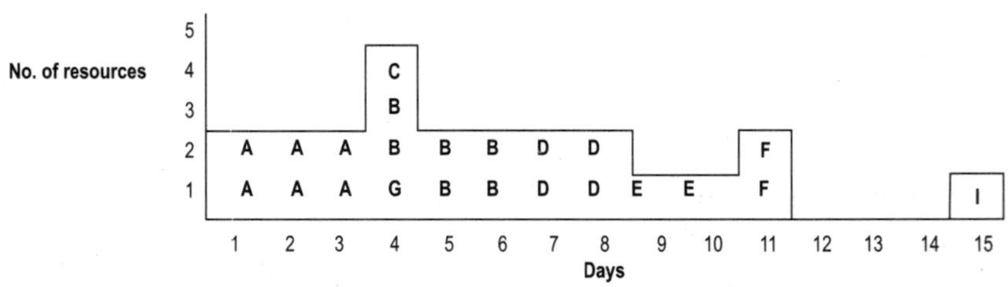

Figure 3.25: Resource histogram for decorating a room.

This diagram, like the Gantt chart, is drawn using the critical path (tasks A, G, H and I) first. Task H, waiting for furniture to be delivered, is a 'dummy' task introduced to make the precedence network more accurate. It does not need any resources to carry it out.

It can now be seen that on day 4 we need four people on the project. If the maximum number of resources available to us is two, then some re-planning needs to occur. The use of the task identifiers in the histogram helps with this. We need to manipulate the tasks in such a way that only 2 resources are used in any one day. Therefore we need to be able to see which tasks are causing a problem, and whether or not they can be moved (ie whether they have any total float). Task B has 3 days of total float so it can be moved to start one day later without much risk, resulting in:

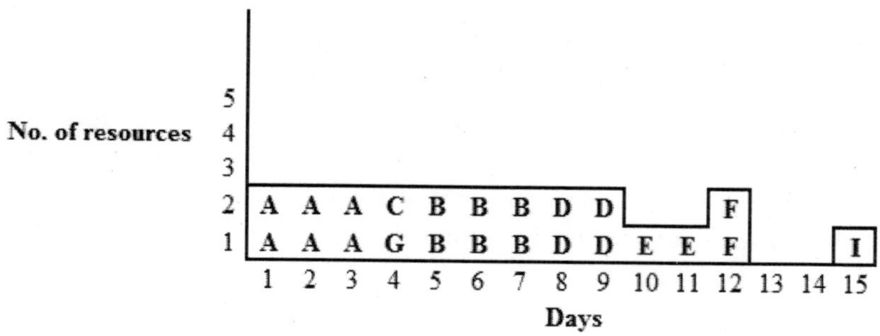

Figure 3.26: Adjusted resource histogram for decorating a room.

Tasks D, E and F have also moved to the right by one day.

This is an example of resource-limited scheduling—scheduling activities so that the maximum resource level is never exceeded during the project. In some cases carrying out resource-limited scheduling will increase the project duration. This is also known as 'resource levelling'.

Time-limited scheduling is scheduling activities so that the maximum project duration is not exceeded. This is not always possible; for example in the decorated room project, if the furniture delivery takes 10 days then there is no way of reducing the project duration to 12 days. This is also known as 'resource smoothing', because the technique uses total float and also possibly varying the number of resources per activity in order to achieve a smooth resource curve. A smooth resource curve is an ideal position for a Project Manager, as it means that the number of resources in the project is not increasing or decreasing rapidly at any point. A spiky resource curve creates management problems because many resources may be joining or leaving the team suddenly.

If you do make any changes to the plan because of scheduling constraints, then these changes need to be reflected in the Gantt chart as well as the resource histogram.

Whether or not you carry out resource-limited or time-limited scheduling depends on constraints imposed on the project, probably by the customer or senior management. The Project Manager has to hope that the project is not tightly constrained by both resources and time!

Assumptions and other narrative

Throughout the planning process it is inevitable that assumptions are made. For example, in the decorated room project we assumed that we could buy the paint in one day, that two people could lay the carpet in one day and that we had the capability in the project team to install the furniture. Any assumptions made are effectively risks to the project, so they need to be documented. A Project Plan is more than just a Gantt chart: it should document all assumptions and any other information that helps the reader to make sense of the plan. This other information will be; a cost breakdown, notes of any external dependencies, exclusions to the scope and interfaces between the work of this project and any other current work.

Impact on the Business Case

Once the Project Plan has been completed, the Business Case must be reviewed for any changes arising out of planning. For example, the project costs and time will probably have changed, and now that we have a better view of assumptions and external dependencies, there may be some significant risks that should be included in the Business Case. Also, the project may now be planned to take longer than was originally predicted, so the achievement of the business benefits in the Business Case may be later than previously estimated.

3.10 Summary

In this chapter you have learnt about the steps in the planning technique:

- ➢ WBS—to show the scope and structure of the work in the project
- ➢ CBS—to illustrate the breakdown of costs
- ➢ OBS—to show the teams and resources to be used to carry out the work
- ➢ RAM—to allocate task responsibilities to the resources
- ➢ Network Diagram—to plot the task dependencies
- ➢ Estimating—to predict the duration of each task
- ➢ Critical Path Analysis—to calculate the project duration and the most critical tasks
- ➢ Gantt Chart—to plot the tasks against the project timescale
- ➢ Resource Histogram—to illustrate the number of resources used against the timescale.

The next chapter shows you how to set up a project organisation structure, to ensure that there is a clear set of roles, responsibilities and communication lines in order to carry out the plan you have just put together.

3.11 Practical assignment

Using section A.3, Information for Project Planning in Appendix A, go through the planning steps for the restaurant project and produce the following:

- WBS
- CBS

- OBS
- RAM
- Network Diagram and Critical Path Analysis
- Gantt Chart
- Resource Histogram
- Assumptions, external dependencies and exclusions.

3.12 Study

Answer the following multiple-choice questions. For answers see Appendix C.

1. What is the purpose of a Work Breakdown Structure?
   a) To show the dependencies between tasks in a project
   b) To illustrate the scope of work included in a project
   c) To ensure that all resources in a project have enough to do
   d) To enable the riskiest activities to be identified

2. How is a Responsibility Assignment Matrix developed?
   a) Using data from the WBS
   b) Using data from the OBS and CBS
   c) Using data from the Precedence Network and OBS
   d) Using data from the WBS and OBS

3. Identify the critical path in the following network (which shows the duration of each task):

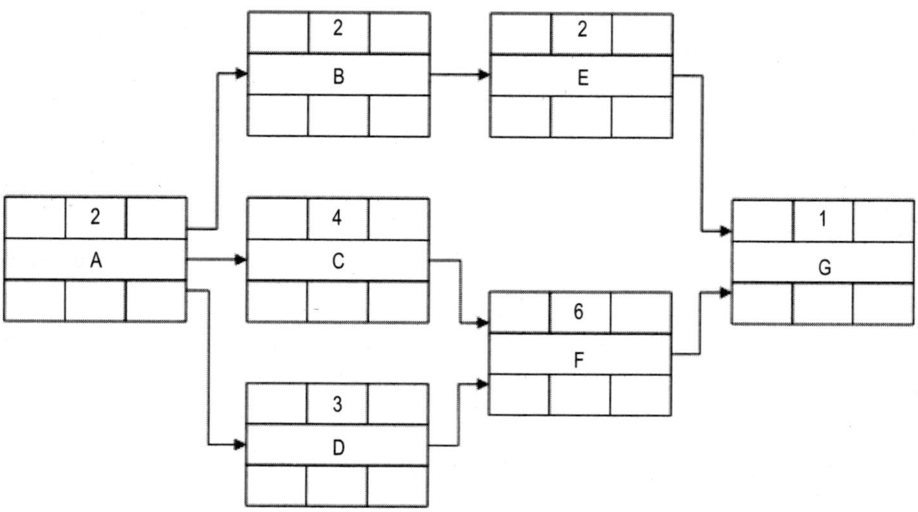

   a) ABEG
   b) ACFG
   c) ADEG
   d) ADFG

4. The critical path is:
   a) The shortest path through the network
   b) The path with most total float
   c) The path with most activities
   d) The longest path through the network

5. What is free float?
   a) The amount by which an activity can be late without affecting the next activity
   b) The amount an activity can be late without affecting the project end date
   c) Float which can applied freely by the Project Manager
   d) Total float minus 1

6. What might result from carrying out time-limited scheduling?
   a) A longer critical path
   b) A reduction in resources required by the project
   c) An increase in resources required by the project
   d) Improved quality.

The project manager's diary

The Project Plan took a long time; getting all of the estimates prepared and sussing out the dependencies were tricky tasks. For example, we could start testing the menus before we've generated all the ideas, but to keep things simple I've left 'Test Menus' as totally dependent on 'Generate Ideas' so that if we do gain a little time, it works as a bit of extra float in the plan. It's important to get these as right as possible because the first plan I show Charlie will doubtlessly be the one he remembers and uses against me later on when things may have slipped. But once I'd got those together I really enjoyed plotting the network diagram and creating the Gantt chart. I'm happy with the resulting plan; Charlie wants the project finished within 6 months and the plan shows we can meet the launch date by 13th May, 30 working days early. From my perspective that 30 days is excellent—plenty of float in my plan in case things get badly delayed, it removes some stress from my shoulders.

Cost-wise I've got less leeway. Charlie wants the whole thing done for £210K and I've estimated the technical work of the project at £185K. I've still got to add the costs of Project Management, risk mitigation and allowances for changes and contingency. It might be tight.

The critical path has emerged from the network diagram as the path containing the engagement of the builders and all of the building work. This is quite worrying as good builders around here are notoriously difficult to find. I used McTavish on the last project and they originally delivered 3 weeks early. But after they had to rebuild the wall that was not properly supported we were 5 weeks late and £25K over budget. I've updated the Risk Log accordingly, and now that I know the project timescale I can update the Business Case with this. I'm going to put contractor search as an immediate priority on the project Plan.

I'm concerned about people management as the resource histogram shows that for a large part of the project I'm going to be managing 9 or 10 people at once. I need to sort out some Team Managers to take some of this workload from me.

Charlie has said he wants some celebrities to attend the launch event, but I'm not really sure what constitutes a 'celebrity' these days. I can't imagine us enticing Premiership footballers or TV personalities. We may end up with some of the local Second Division football team or some reality TV 'personalities'. This needs definition if I'm going to deliver what Charlie wants.

4 Project organisation: Establishing effective teams and reporting lines

This chapter describes the different roles required in a project team and the responsibilities of each role. Many projects fail because the people chosen for a role do not understand it or are not really experienced enough to be able to carry it out properly. All structured Project Management methods rely on the organisation structure working seamlessly, where each individual is accountable for his or her own tasks and there are no responsibilities left unassigned. This chapter outlines these roles and responsibilities so that you can make sure the right people with the right abilities are selected for your project organisation structure.

In the last chapter, you developed an Organisational Breakdown Structure (OBS) for the Restaurant Case Study. That OBS was a hierarchy of technical people managed ultimately by the Project Manager. This chapter deals with the full Project Management team, so covers the responsibilities of the management roles in the project as well as the technical ones.

It is useful to have a model of a project organisation structure that works for the smallest project, the largest project and every size of project in between. So for that reason the 'roles' in the project team are described, rather than the 'people'. Most

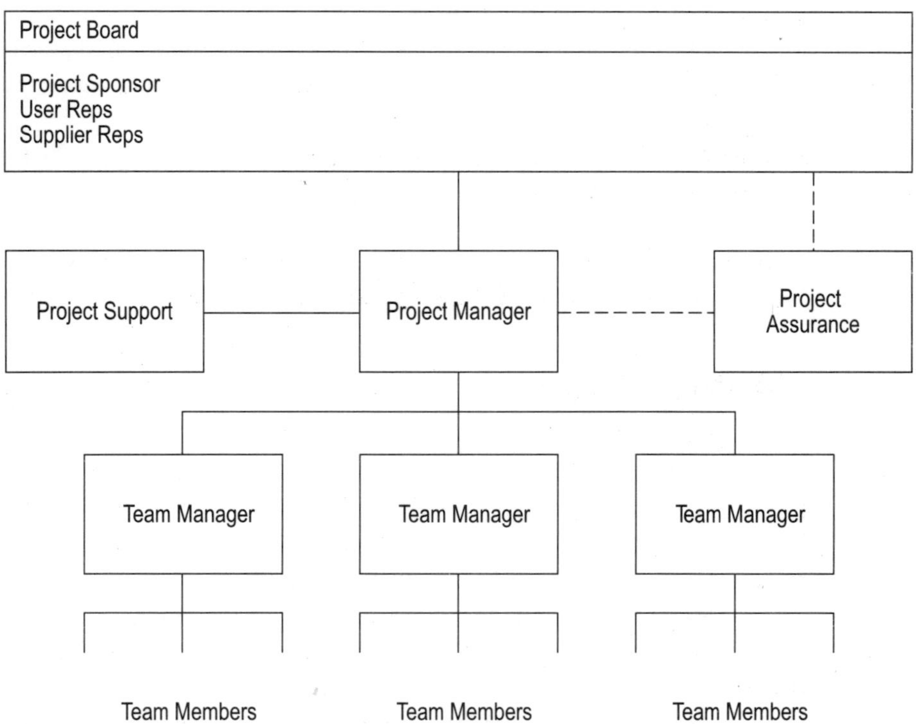

Figure 4.1: Project organisation structure.

roles can be populated by more than one person, and a person can take on more than one role.

The project organisation structure model is shown in Figure 4.1.

We will use an example of a small IT project to illustrate the way in which the organisation is put together. Suppose that a company, Wobbly Widgets, which manufactures and sells widgets, has recognised the need to update its website in order to improve sales. The company has an internal IT department which will carry out the development work.

4.1 Project Manager

The Project Manager is responsible for the day-to-day management of the project. As described in Chapter 1, the Project Manager's job is to get the project completed within the constraints of time, cost and quality, according to the 'contract' between the Project Manager and the Project Sponsor, i.e., the Project Management Plan.

There should be only one person in the role of Project Manager. The Project Manager needs to make decisions about the day-to-day management of the project, is the focus for communication around the project and takes responsibility for the planning and other documentation. He writes the Project Management Plan under the supervision of the Project Sponsor, and owns the Project Management Plan throughout the project.

It is usual for the Project Manager to be someone who works for the customer organisation. This is because the Project Manager will be motivated to:

- Complete the project within the constraints of time and cost
- Ensure that the project's products are thoroughly tested to fulfil the specification
- Ensure that the project's products are successfully implemented within the customer organisation
- Keep the Business Case, which may be a commercially sensitive product, up-to-date (checking on cost variations and reviewing pressures for change).

In our example project, the Project Manager will be someone who works for Wobbly Widgets and ideally has good Project Management experience.

4.2 Project Sponsor

The Project Sponsor is the 'champion' of the project; responsible for driving the project forward in the customer organisation, providing the funding and ensuring that the business benefits of the project will be realised.

There should be only one person in the role of Project Sponsor. This is because the Project Sponsor is the one role ultimately accountable for the success of the project.

The Project Sponsor takes the 'business' view of the project. This means that, in terms of decision-making, the Project Sponsor should always make the decision that is best for the business, which may not necessarily be the best decision for the users or for the suppliers. For example, the Project Sponsor may decide to reject a suggestion for an improvement to a product, on the basis that the benefits the improvement will bring to the users are outweighed by the cost of the improvement. The users may not be happy with this as they are mainly concerned about the products that they will ultimately use, and the suppliers will usually want to carry out the improvement as they would normally receive payment for making it.

As the Project Sponsor is the key decision-maker on the project, he needs to be a senior person, well-respected within the customer organisation with authority, good business skills and an understanding of finance. Usually he will be someone at Director level within the customer organisation.

The Project Sponsor will either write the Business Case or oversee the Project Manager writing it, and will approve the Project Management Plan.

As the updated website is very important to Wobbly Widgets, the Project Sponsor could be the Managing Director.

4.3 Project Board

The Project Board is a group of people who direct the project and represent key parties involved. The Project Sponsor may be the chair of the Project Board, or may be separate from it. The Project Board should contain people who represent the ultimate users of the project's products and also those who are supplying the products. This means that decisions made will incorporate the views of the main parties and any conflicts can be resolved by this group.

The User Rep will ensure that the project delivers what the end users require, and will allocate user resources to the project when they are required, typically during requirements specification, acceptance testing and training. The Supplier Rep will allocate supplier resources to the project and ensure that the work is done correctly and to standards.

The Project Board is also sometimes known as the Steering Group.

In the Project Board in our example project, a sensible choice of User Rep would be the Sales Director, as the website is a sales tool. The Supplier Rep would be the IT Director, as he is supplying the technical resources (software developers) to the project.

4.4 Team Managers

Team Managers report to the Project Manager and supervise the team of people actually carrying out the development activities on a day-to-day basis.

Team Managers need more detailed and technical knowledge than the Project Manager, as they will plan, monitor and control the work of each team member.

Team Manager is an optional role; on a very small project the Project Manager might be the person overseeing all of the technical work, or there may be only two or three technical team members and the Project Manager can manage them directly.

In the Wobbly Widgets project, there will be a Team Manager from IT who supervises the team developing and implementing the updated website, and a Team Manager from the Sales department who will supervise the team of salespeople specifying the website requirements and carrying out the user testing, and will ensure that all of the sales team are trained in the use of the new website.

4.5 Project Support

Project Support is another optional role. On a large project, the Project Manager will be kept very busy by the tasks of Project Management, and will have very little time for administration of the project. It is invaluable to have someone, or a group of people, who can take the administrative workload away from the Project Manager. So Project Support will carry out tasks such as filing, arranging meetings, taking minutes and possibly updating plans on the basis of progress information received from the teams.

In our example project, the Project Manager may be able to do his or her own support as it is quite a small project. Otherwise the role could be fulfilled by anyone in the Wobbly Widgets organisation who has a general knowledge of projects and good organisation and administration skills.

4.6 Project Assurance

This role may also be known as Project Audit. It is the responsibility of the Project Board to assure that everything about the project is on track, that there are not going to be any (nasty) surprises and that the business benefits are going to be achieved. But on a large project, the Project Board may not have enough time to assure the project in this way, so they can bring in someone else (or a team) to carry this out on their behalf.

Some of the activities that the Project Assurance role will carry out are:

- Providing advice and guidance to the Project Manager on all aspects of the project
- Reviewing documents and plans before the Project Manager sends them to the Project Board
- Checking that the project documentation is accurate and that the project is on track
- Providing a sounding-board to the Project Manager in respect of project Issues
- Checking that everyone involved in the project understands his role and responsibilities.

It can be useful for this role to be filled by someone external to the customer organisation, as it can be difficult for someone constrained by company politics to be honest about the situation if things aren't really going as well as is believed.

In the new website project, the role of Project Assurance may well be carried out by the Project Board as it is a fairly small project. Alternatively, the Project Sponsor may decide that the project is so crucial for the business that someone else should carry this out. If Wobbly Widgets has a Quality Assurance team, specifying the standards that the organisation works to, then someone from that team could be brought into the project team to carry out Project Assurance.

This project organisation model works for any size of project. For a small project the optional roles of Team Managers and Project Support may not be used, and the Project Assurance role will be performed by the Project Board. On a very large project, all roles except the Project Sponsor and Project Manager may be fulfilled by a team of people.

> "No institution can possibly survive if it needs geniuses or supermen to manage it. It must be organised in such a way as to be able to get along under a leadership composed of average human beings."
> Peter F. Drucker 1909 (American management guru)

4.7 Summary

In this chapter you have learnt:

- A generic model of a project organisation structure
- The main roles and responsibilities in the project organisation.

The next chapter describes the purpose and importance of stakeholder management. This helps to keep everyone involved in the project informed and motivated.

4.8 Practical assignment

Design the Project Organisation Structure for the restaurant project, based on the OBS you developed in Chapter 3 and using the information in Appendix A.

4.9 Study

Answer the following multiple-choice questions. For answers see Appendix C.

1. Which is the best description of the Project Sponsor?
   a) The user representative
   b) The supplier representative
   c) The project champion
   d) Day-to-day manager.

2. Who owns the Project Management Plan?
   a) The Project Manager and teams
   b) The Project Sponsor
   c) The Project Board
   d) Project Assurance.

3. What is the maximum number of people in a Project Management team?
   a) Seven
   b) Five
   c) Twenty
   d) There is no maximum.

4. Who probably writes the Business Case?
   a) Project Assurance
   b) The Project Manager, under the direction of the Project Sponsor
   c) Project Support
   d) The Project Board.

The project manager's diary

Well, today was undoubtedly my hardest day on the project so far. We had a meeting to sort out the Org Structure with the intention of getting all the project roles and responsibilities sorted out. I wanted to push for actually getting lists of responsibilities signed off by the team so that I could hold them accountable for their jobs; the organisation structure underpins the Project Management processes in a project.

Persuading Charlie that the Project Board owns the project and is accountable for its ultimate success was a nightmare. He kept saying, "But that's what I pay you for." As patiently as I could, I outlined the reasons why the authority making all of the major decisions on the project had to be the one held accountable. For example, I can't make decisions about equipment specification because I don't understand how to cook crispy duck and so I need input from him. Finally, we reached a compromise whereby he makes the decisions but I keep him informed as much as possible. We shall see if he really wants to be bothered with the minutiae of a project on a day-to-day basis.

After this tussle and my partial victory, when Charlie said that there was no way he was going to pay for a Project Support person to assist me with administration and filing, I had to concede this and agree to do it myself. I wasn't happy about also carrying out the tasks of configuration control, but I could see that there might not be enough support work to justify a full-time salary.

So the Organisation is agreed, now I need to ensure that we get some really good people to fill those roles. I'll start talking to the local recruitment agencies about the catering staff.

5 Stakeholder management: Keeping everyone informed and positive

This chapter describes how to manage the expectations of all those interested in the project. Once those interests have been understood, a plan can be developed which will help to keep those interested parties appropriately informed and positive about the project's outcome.

The suppliers in a project are one of the parties most impacted by the project. So this chapter also deals with the topic of procuring goods or services from suppliers, and different ways to pay them.

A specific stakeholder that Project Managers need to be aware of is the Health and Safety Executive (HSE). The key activities that a Project Manager needs to carry out in order to satisfy this organisation are covered.

In the last chapter, we described the roles of those people actively involved in the project and modelled them in a Project Organisation. Apart from those actively involved, there are also organisations and people who will be impacted by the project in some way. It is important to consider these parties as they may influence the outcome of the project.

Any person or organisation with an interest in the project is known as a 'stakeholder'. Stakeholders may have a positive or negative interest in the project. For example, a project to build a house on an empty plot of land will have an impact on those living nearby. Some of those neighbours may be pleased that the land is going to be occupied, but others may prefer it to remain empty and may object to the planning permission application that you put forward to the local council.

> "I think the hardest thing about my job is the way Whole Foods Market views itself philosophically is that we are a business dedicated to meeting all the various stakeholders of the company's best interests. And by stakeholders we mean customers, team members, stockholders, community, and the environment. Sometimes what is in the best interest of one stakeholder may not be in the best interest of another stakeholder, and as the CEO, I have to balance the various interests of the different constituencies and stakeholders to create win, win, win scenarios, and that can sometimes be very difficult to do. Everybody wants something from the CEO."
>
> John Mackey (Chairman and CEO of Whole Foods Market)

5.1 Stakeholder analysis

The first step in stakeholder management is to analyse the stakeholders. This starts with identifying them, which may be best achieved by a brainstorming session with other team members. The key thing is to consider everyone who has an interest in, or is impacted by, the project.

Once each stakeholder is identified, the factors to consider for each one are the level of support and the level of influence that each has for the project. These can then be plotted on a Stakeholder Mapping Grid, with each of the two factors being scored Low, Medium or High:

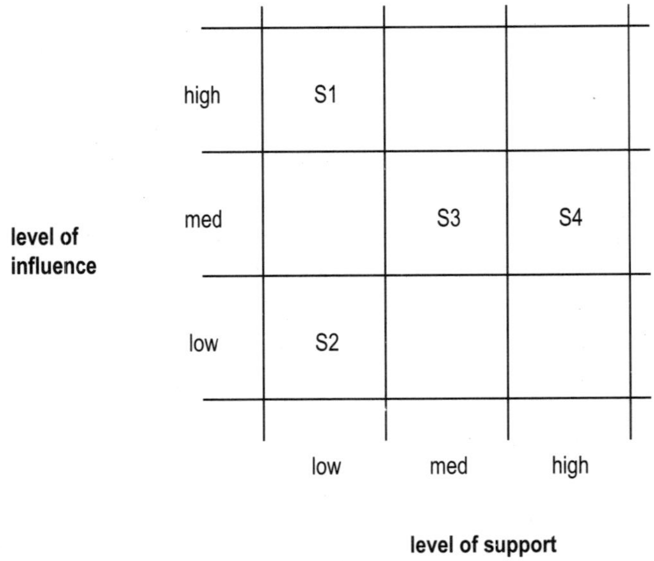

Figure 5.1: Stakeholder mapping grid.

So in Figure 5.1 above, 'S1' refers to Stakeholder 1, who has a low level of support for the project but a high level of influence. In the example of building a house, this could be a council planning application officer who wants to retain green fields in the area. One of the objectives of stakeholder management is to work out how to get Stakeholder 1 moved across this grid so that the level of support is increased. There may also be something that we could do about their level of influence, but this is not always possible, because usually someone's level of influence is determined by their position of authority.

Stakeholder 2 has a low level of support for the project but also has a low level of influence. For example, this could be a local environmental group in the area where you want to build the new house. It would be helpful to persuade this stakeholder of some reasons why the project may be beneficial to him and thus move him across the Stakeholder Mapping Grid, but as he has a low level of influence this is probably not crucial to the project.

Stakeholder 3 has a medium level of both influence and support. For example, this could be the people currently living next door to the plot of land. They could be fairly ambivalent about the prospect of having new next door neighbours, and the local council will take some notice of their views. Again, influencing this stakeholder may not be crucial to the project's success, but it could be quite important to maintain their level of support as 'medium' rather than allowing it to drop to 'low'.

Stakeholder 4 is highly supportive of the project but has a medium level of influence. For example, this could be the building firm that you are thinking of contracting to build your house. As they have a high level of support already, it is not worth spending much time trying to influence them. But they should appear in the project Communication Plan as they need to be kept informed and will provide the project with useful information about progress and problems.

What we have determined so far is that each of these stakeholders has different success criteria for the project. Success criteria are the measures by which a stakeholder will determine whether the project was a success. So, for example, in Chapter 1 we saw that the success criteria for a Project Manager were the delivery of the project within the constraints of time, cost and quality. Success criteria for the Project Sponsor will be the realisation of the business benefits in the Business Case. The success criteria for the building firm who are hoping to be contracted by you, will be that they make a good profit from the contract.

Success factors are the items that are put into place to assist the achievement of the success criteria. So for a Project Manager, the success factors are having all of the essential elements of Project Management implemented successfully in the project environment. For example, having set up and used good risk management, good communication...basically the topics covered by this book are the success factors for a Project Manager. For the Project Sponsor, success factors will be keeping the focus on the Business Case throughout the project, updating it, and referring to it at all key points to ensure achievement of the business benefits.

The next step of stakeholder analysis is to assess the success criteria of each stakeholder. Then we can work out the appropriate success factors and put these into the project—this may mean altering the project objectives.

So in the house-building example, the list of stakeholders, Success Criteria and Success Factors may look like this:

No.	Stakeholder	Success Criteria	Success Factors
1	Council officer	Project only goes ahead if carbon neutral. Conforms to local policies.	Have solar panels.
2	Local environmental group	No negative environmental impact.	Have a wind turbine. Generate all own power.
3	Next door neighbour	House looks nice. Minimal disruption. No overlooking.	Ask neighbours' opinion on design. Ensure no disruption from the builders.
4	Potential building firm	Project goes ahead and our building firm is used.	

Figure 5.2: Stakeholders, Success Criteria and Success Factors.

It may be that, once we talk to the council officer, he will be persuaded to approve the application if we put solar panels into the design, as he is very keen on projects that are carbon neutral. Similarly, the local environmental group may be influenced positively about the project if we agree to generate all of our own power and install a wind turbine. The next door neighbours may be more supportive of the project if we consult them about the design of the house, and can guarantee that the builders will be very careful not to disrupt them during the building work. It is up to the building firm to put into place their own success factors for securing the business with the customer organisation.

> "The two most important parts of a computing system are the users and their data, in that order."
> Neville Holmes (*Computer*, Nov 2004)

5.2 Stakeholder management

The success factors that have been determined by stakeholder analysis now need to be put into place to ensure that they happen. This means adding actions into the Project Plan and developing a Communication Plan.

The Communication Plan is the result of determining the appropriate information, communication method and frequency of communication for each stakeholder. This will help to keep each stakeholder involved in the project, with the intention of maintaining or even improving their level of support.

The Communication Plan is usually in the form of a table, where for each stakeholder, the following is identified:

- Information needs: what information should be provided to this stakeholder
- Communication methods: what is the best way to provide this information to this stakeholder
- Timing: frequency of the communication
- Responsibilities: who will obtain the information and provide it to the stakeholder
- Feedback routes: how will we capture and respond to the stakeholder's comments.

The Communication Plan should be monitored throughout the project, and should be changed if the strategy for managing the stakeholders is not working successfully.

5.3 Procurement

As already mentioned, suppliers are one of the key stakeholders in any project. Suppliers may be internal to, or external from, the customer organisation. If they are external, then the process of selecting and contracting with them needs to be considered.

Procurement has a set of specific steps:

- **Requirements**
  This is developing a specification of what it is we require from a supplier. It is usually done in the Definition phase.
- **Requisition**
  This step involves evaluating the potential sources of supply, usually based on a set of pre-defined criteria. It may include putting together a 'bid pack' (a set of information to assist each bidder) and possibly holding a bidder conference, if the project is very large.

- **Solicitation**
  This step involves the selection of possible suppliers and negotiation of terms and conditions, once the information out of the Requisition step (i.e., bids from suppliers) has been received.
- **Award**
  This is the last step and results in a signed contract between the customer and supplier.

If the project you are undertaking includes a significant amount of procured goods or services, then these procurement steps should be added into the Project Plan. Procurement can be a costly and time-consuming activity for both the customer and the supplier, and estimates of the effort required to procure goods or services should always be generous.

5.4 Contract types

At some point in the Procurement process, the customer needs to decide what sort of contract he prefers to use. The main contract types are:

- **Comprehensive**
  In a comprehensive contract, one supplier takes responsibility for delivery of everything required. This can also include management of any other suppliers, if the main supplier sub-contracts some of the work to other suppliers. So the main supplier takes most of the risk, and the customer has only limited access to any sub-contractors.
- **Sequenced**
  This is the term used when more than one supplier is contracted by the customer, in a sequential manner. For example, a customer may use one supplier for the business analysis work, then another supplier for the design work. It is a useful way of working when the requirements are not well known, as it carries less risk than contracting the whole project to one supplier.
- **Parallel**
  In a project where more than one supplier is to be used, if the customer manages relationships with all suppliers, then the contracts run in parallel. The customer has more access to the suppliers than in a comprehensive contract, and will spend a lot more time and effort in supplier management. The customer may well end up managing the interfaces between suppliers, so usually takes on more risk than the suppliers.

As well as different contract types, there are different ways of defining how the supplier will be paid.

5.5 Payment terms

- **Fixed price (or lump sum)**
  The price is fixed, except for variations in contract (change requests). So the customer knows exactly how much he will pay the supplier. This implies that the risk lies with the supplier, so usually the supplier will put a significant margin into any fixed price quote to cover this risk.

- **Unit rate**
  The price is based on units of work done, or on resources used. This is also known as 'T&M' (time and materials). The risk usually lies with the customer because if the scope of the project increases, the price will increase, and also because the time taken to complete a task is within the supplier's control. The supplier will usually quote day rates for certain resources, with margins already built into those rates. The supplier has no opportunity of making a very large profit, as they might with fixed price, but equally has no risk of making a loss.
- **Cost-reimbursement**
  In this payment type, the customer pays all the supplier costs of people and materials. This would imply that the supplier makes no margin at all. In fact, this payment type is often used for only a part of the total supply, such as materials. For example, if you employ a decorator he will often supply the paint to the project at cost, but charge you a day rate for his labour. There is also 'cost plus', which is used a great deal in construction projects where the customer will pay (say) 10% added to the total costs.

  In both of these payment methods, there can be problems agreeing what represents 'real' costs to the supplier.
- **Retention money**
  This is where the customer retains some proportion of the payment until the goods or services are proved to conform to the customer's requirements. This retention period could be quite long, perhaps even a year for a large IT or construction project. This reduces the risk to the customer.
- **Liquidated damages**
  Liquidated damages in a contract means that the customer will pay less for the goods or services if damages have been incurred because of delays or problems caused by the supplier. The reimbursement is intended to offset the damages that have been incurred. In practice, this amount is often estimated at the time of signing the contract. For example, if the project is constructing a building, it is usually easy to determine the cost of delay as this is often the reduced rental incomes or reduced profits for the customer. So a figure is agreed, say £1,000 per week for non-completion to the required standard fit for occupation.

5.6 Health and Safety

The Health and Safety Executive is one of the key stakeholders in many projects, and especially in construction projects. It has a significant amount of influence as it can close down the project if proper procedures are not being followed. This is not the same for an IT project where the teams are working at their desks producing software. But the issue of Health and Safety has to be recognised by all Project Managers, to a greater or lesser extent. Even software developers may be at risk from Health and Safety Issues. For example, loose cables across the floor or filing cabinet drawers left open represent a hazard. Every Project Manager needs to understand the key points of the Health and Safety at Work Act and what this means to their project.

The Health and Safety at Work Act covers two main areas: the responsibilities of the employer, and those of the employee.

The Employer's Duty of Care means that the employer is responsible for providing the following:

- A safe place of work and safe access for employees
- Safe working practices and adequate materials
- Competent fellow employees
- Employees aware of their own responsibilitie
- Protection of the public at large.

The responsibilities of each employee are to:

- Follow guidelines and report all Issues
- Stay within competence levels
- Not misuse any equipment
- Take personal responsibility for his or her own health and safety.

The Project Manager is an employee (or consultant) but also represents the employer to the teams, so needs to be aware of both sets of responsibilities and to advise appropriate action.

5.7 Summary

In this chapter you have learnt:

➢ How to analyse stakeholders
➢ Why a Communication Plan is important in stakeholder management
➢ The benefits of stakeholder management
➢ The types of contract and payment terms that may be used
➢ The importance of Health and Safety in all projects.

The next chapter shows how to manage project risks. This will reduce the chances of those things that may go wrong in your project from having a significant effect, and to increase the opportunities for things going better than you have predicted.

5.8 Practical assignment

Carry out Stakeholder Analysis for the restaurant project, and produce a Communication Plan.

5.9 Study

Answer the following multiple-choice questions. For answers see Appendix C.

1. Stakeholders are:
   a) Users
   b) Suppliers

c) Project Sponsor
d) All of the above, plus more.

2. What is the first step of stakeholder management?
   a) Stakeholder analysis
   b) Stakeholder assessment
   c) Stakeholder influence mapping
   d) Stakeholder support mapping.

3. What is the purpose of a Communication Plan?
   a) To ensure all forms of communication are used
   b) To ensure that all stakeholders are kept informed about the project
   c) To monitor continually a stakeholder's level of support
   d) To ensure regular meetings involving everyone in the Organisational Breakdown Structure (OBS).

4. Which type of contract means that the primary supplier manages all of the other suppliers simultaneously?
   a) Parallel
   b) Sequenced
   c) Comprehensive
   d) Liquidated damages.

The project manager's diary

Charlie and I sat down today to review what I'd come up with for stakeholder analysis. Fortunately the only stakeholders with a potentially negative view of the project are the local residents, the local council and the HSE. Charlie and I both believe that we can win over the local residents with some promotional offers, and once Charlie has chatted up the local council about the planning permission issue, we only have the HSE to worry about, and the Architect and building firm should be pretty familiar with their constraints. Note to self: we still need to be careful because on the McTavish project the HSE shut down the site whilst they investigated why a builder had broken his ankle; it turned out that he'd slipped on some green slimy stuff, probably mould.

For the interior design company I needed to see the project from their perspective to work out their success criteria. They want this project be a flagship for them to gain more customers. They want the interior to be supplied with top-notch accessories and this might conflict with Charlie's cost budget. Made a private note here, on my Risk Log. Often stakeholder analysis needs to be kept confidential as some of it may be contentious—you don't want a stakeholder to see that they are a threat.

When I created the Communication Plan from the stakeholder analysis, there was a lot of discussion about publicity—the issue is that a lot of restaurants have been opening in this town recently due to re-generation, and we need to create a story to get the press interested. I need to make sure that I add actions to the relevant Stage Plan for Charlie and for me to ensure that the publicity works ok. At the moment the Gantt chart just shows 'Advertise launch event' and this will need a lot of fleshing out in order to be an effective plan.

6 Project risk: How to control risks and avoid fire-fighting

This chapter establishes what is meant by risk in the context of a project, outlines a technique for analysing risks, and describes the different actions that can be taken to manage those risks. It sets the scene for managing risks throughout the project, and links the management of risk to the constraints of time and cost.

Risks are part of everyday life and part of every project. Some projects are more risky than others; for example, a project to build a bridge is far riskier than putting up shelves in your study—if the bridge were to fail then people may be killed or injured, but if the shelves were to fail then probably the worst outcome would be some damaged books. In both cases, these risks need to be controlled.

Have you ever felt stressed about the chances of things going wrong in your project? Risk management is all about taking a pro-active approach to managing that uncertainty and gaining a level of control over it. This will give you and your stakeholders a greater level of confidence that the project can be delivered within time, cost and quality constraints, as you have identified the main things that could go wrong and have an action plan to deal with them. This should lead to your working day involving less time managing risk and more time managing the project as a whole. As a result, in your time away from work you will be feeling less stressed about the project.

"To make a mistake is only human; to persist in a mistake is idiotic."
Cicero (Roman orator, politician and philosopher)

6.1 What is risk?

Risk is uncertainty. Project risk is uncertainty in your project. We tend to think of the word 'risk' as relating to things that can go wrong, i.e., that risks are all negative. But in Project Management the word 'risk' relates to all the things that can end up differently from the way they were expected, so risks can be positive as well. For example, if you are decorating a spare room in your house you might consider risks such as the chance of spilling paint on your carpet, or not getting the job done before your relatives arrive needing the spare room, but you should also consider the chance of finishing the job early, or the project costing you less than you had budgeted. For these risks you may have the opportunity to do something else, such as complete one of those DIY jobs you didn't finish last year.

So, risks can be threats or opportunities. We've already mentioned the benefits of managing threats, but why worry about things going better than expected? These opportunities are worth investigating because they can cause you to change your plans and maybe for a small amount of effort you can increase your chances of these opportunities happening. If you can save money on the spare room project, you may be able to afford to buy some items for the room which will further improve it, such as a new mirror. In a larger project, such as building a new house, you may find that spending an extra £2,000 on the kitchen, to make it absolutely stunning, will put £5,000 on the value of the house. What a shame if you were to miss this opportunity. If you are managing an IT project within the organisation you work for, there may be a chance of delivering it a few weeks early, in which case you might be able to avoid renewing a maintenance contract. So the forecast benefit of the opportunity may outweigh the cost of taking advantage of the opportunity.

Risks are potential variations to future planned events, not certainties. If a risk occurs, it is no longer a risk but something that needs to be dealt with immediately by the Project Manager. These events are described in Chapter 10, Project Controls.

6.2 What is risk management?

Risk Management is a process that lays out the key steps of managing risks so that the Project Manager has better control over them. It aims to make the most of opportunities for increasing the success of the project, and to avoid or reduce threats to the project's success. All projects contain risk, so risk management is a crucial process. It is the Project Manager's responsibility to ensure that risk management is carried out properly and effectively.

6.3 The risk management process

The steps in risk management are:

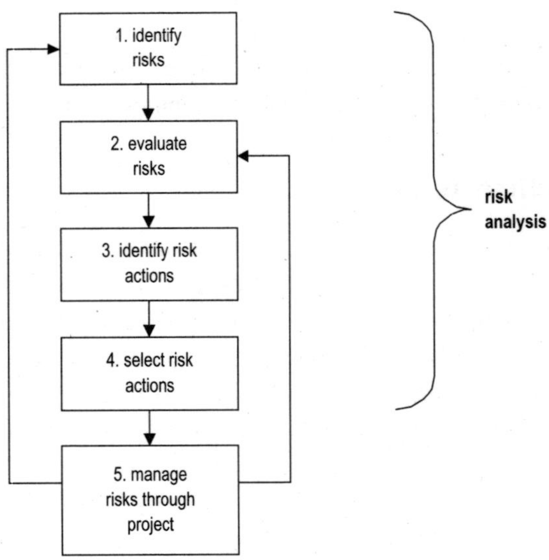

Figure 6.1: Processing steps in the management of risk.

The first four of these steps are known as 'risk analysis'. The output of risk analysis is a completed Risk Log, which is the register of all risks, their assessment and action plans.

The production and maintenance of the Risk Log is a key activity for the Project Manager and ensures that a record is kept of all actions and decisions about the risks. Some risk analysis will be carried out in the Conception phase of the project in order to indetify any 'show-stoppers' in the Business Case, but full risk analysis is carried out mainly in the Definition phase of the project. The diagram shows the iterative nature of the management of risk, i.e., when the project is in the Implementation phase, and you are managing the risks proactively using action plans, you may identify new risks and should re-visit risks to re-assess them. Risks change throughout the project and need to be reviewed regularly.

6.3.1 Identify risks

Former US Defence Secretary Donald Rumsfeld won a 'Foot in Mouth' award from the British Plain English Campaign for his comments at a news conference in February 2002 when he said, "Reports that say that something hasn't happened are always interesting to me, because as we know, there are known knowns; there are things we know we know. We also know there are known unknowns; that is to say we know there are some things we do not know. But there are also unknown unknowns—the ones we don't know we don't know."

While the rest of the world laughed, Project Managers tried to hide their embarrassment because they actually knew what he meant. 'Things we know we know' are certainties—not risks. The point of risk identification is to take the 'unknown unknowns' and turn them into 'known unknowns' and then we can have some control over them. Things that remain as 'unknown unknowns' are those things you haven't even thought about.

You need to be pragmatic about the risks you try to control. Some risks will have a very low likelihood—consider risks such as floods and earthquakes. These will obviously have a serious impact, but in most organisations they are covered by disaster recovery plans or insurance. If they are not covered already, and your project involves building something on a flood plain, then you do need to include them. You need to apply common sense to these sorts of risks.

Here are some methods of identifying risks:

- Brainstorming with the project team
- Identifying assumptions
- Using Lessons Learned reports from previous projects
- Looking at the project documentation already produced, such as the Business Case and Project Plan
- Interviewing stakeholders
- Reviewing the strengths and weaknesses of the project.

Brainstorming

This is a creative technique to generate ideas to solve a problem. You could hold a workshop where the project team identifies as many risks as possible. In the true spirit of brainstorming, no idea is a bad one, and you know that you are going to assess each risk afterwards, so you can encourage creativity and lateral thinking. The Project Manager cannot really be expected to identify all risks on a project as a solitary exercise carried out in front of a computer. Team members will have varying views of the project. For example, technical people will come up with risks that are quite different from those identified by financial people.

Assumptions

Every assumption generates a risk. For example, in your Project Plan you may have assumed that a particular person, who is an expert in a specialist technical area, will be available to work on your project. The project may be put into jeopardy if you rely on this and then it turns out that the person is not available.

Lessons learned

Every Project Manager should produce a Lessons Learned Report when closing down a project. We will cover this in more detail in Chapter 12: Handover and Closeout. It is always useful to review Lessons Learned Reports from other projects, especially projects similar to the one you are undertaking. These may hold useful information about what sorts of risks actually occurred on previous projects.

Documentation

The documentation you have produced so far can highlight risks. For example, the Responsibility Matrix will indicate if you are heavily dependent on one resource to do a lot of the work, and the Network Diagram shows the Critical Path through the project.

Interviews

Some stakeholders may not attend the risk brainstorming workshop, or some of the risks they want to raise might be politically sensitive. For instance, a new system may cause the organisation to consider redundancies in order to save salary costs. So a structured interview with a stakeholder may be the appropriate way to identify these risks.

Strengths and weaknesses

The strengths and weaknesses of the project can be used to identify opportunities and threats. For example, the project team may be very experienced in the technical work of the project and so you may see an opportunity to bring the project in ahead of schedule. Or there may be a technical skill that is missing from the project team, and this threatens the project's delivery.

6.3.2 Assess risks

Once you have identified risks, the next step is to evaluate them. This enables the Project Manager to decide whether it is worth carrying out any actions to minimise the threats and maximise the opportunities, or whether the risk is quite insignificant so spending time (and therefore money) on it is not worthwhile. Risk assessment (also known as 'evaluation') is the scoring of each risk on two scales: probability and impact.

Probability

The probability of a risk is the likelihood of its happening. For example, the likelihood of your car breaking down will be affected by such factors as its age and whether you have had it serviced recently.

Impact

The impact of a risk is how significant the effect on the project will be, if it does happen. For example, if your car does break down, the impact on you will depend on things like whether you have breakdown cover and the importance of the journey you are making. It is useful to consider how much the risk will impact on the project in terms of time (will it affect the end date?), cost (will it increase or decrease the budget?) and quality (will it impact on the quality of the finished products?). This is the time, cost and quality triangle as discussed in Chapter 1; see Figure 1.2. As these are the three main targets for the Project Manager, it makes sense to consider each risk in terms of these.

For both probability and impact, a sensible way of scoring them is in terms of low, medium or high. Once these are scored, you can show the results in a Risk Assessment Grid:

impact				
	high 3	3	6	9
	med 2	2	4	6
	low 1	1	2	3
		1 low	2 med	3 high
			probability	

Figure 6.2: Risk Assessment Grid.

If low is 1, medium is 2 and high is 3, then multiplying out the scores on the axes means that a high probability, high impact risk is scored as a 9. A low probability, low impact risk scores 1, and so on.

A useful aspect of the Risk Assessment Grid is that you can plot the Risk No. of each risk in the appropriate box, and then gain a view of the level of risk for the project—are there many numbers in the top-right corner of the grid, or are most of them in the bottom left corner, or somewhere in between? If you have many risks in the top right corner, then the project appears to have many significant risks. The project has fewer, smaller risks if there are just a few numbers plotted in the bottom left area, and hardly any numbers elsewhere in the grid.

The threats in the top right corner are more likely to need mitigating, whereas those in the bottom left corner may be threats that you accept without any management actions. The pattern is the same for opportunities. The opportunities in the top right corner are those that are most likely to be worth investing time and money in, and those in the bottom left corner are possibly not worth any effort.

Sometimes the Risk Assessment Grid uses a 5 by 5 matrix instead of the 3 by 3 matrix in figure 6.2. This implies that probability and impact are scored as very low, low, medium, high or very high. This more detailed risk evaluation may be useful in situations where you are able to differentiate between (say) low and very low.

6.3.3 Identify risk actions

The next step is to identify possible actions that could be taken for each risk that needs managing. There are different actions available, depending on whether the risk is an opportunity or a threat.

Actions for threats: Prevent

If a threat is significant, consider preventing it. This means removing it as a possible risk. For example, if you are travelling a long way to an important meeting that starts at 9am, you would probably prevent the risk of being late due to traffic delays by staying the night before in a local hotel.

Actions for threats: Reduce

Reducing a threat means reducing the probability or the impact. In the case of the risk of being late for a meeting, you could reduce the probability by setting off earlier. You could reduce the impact of being late by ensuring that someone else at the meeting can represent you if you are late.

Actions for threats: Transfer

Transferring a threat transfers the impact of it to another party. A good illustration of risk transference is taking out car insurance, as it transfers the risk of damage to another car to your insurance company. This doesn't affect the probability of the risk, but your insurance company accepts responsibility for this risk and any financial impact. There needs to be a contractual agreement between you and your insurance company for them to acknowledge this risk.

Actions for threats: Accept

Accepting a threat is a positive decision to do nothing. The risk may have been assessed with a low score, or there may not be anything that you can reasonably do about it. For example, you may decide to live with the risk that you are late for the meeting, on the basis that nothing useful was to be covered in the first hour.

Actions for threats: Contingency

A contingency plan will only be carried out if a risk actually occurs, so this action is the 'plan B'. So if you do get caught in traffic, then you could phone the chairperson of the meeting and he could re-arrange the agenda to move the items that concern you to later on in the meeting.

Actions for opportunities: Share

Sharing an opportunity means using some kind of bonus or incentive. If you have invested in a project to build a house with the intention of selling the house immediately, you may recognise the opportunity to sell the house for more than you predicted in your Business Case. You could share this opportunity by offering 10% of the difference between the actual sale price and the predicted sale price to the builder, as an incentive for him to deliver the highest standard of work.

Actions for opportunities: Ignore

This is the 'do nothing' option for opportunities. Maybe the opportunity is too small to warrant spending any time or money on it, or there is nothing you can reasonably do to increase the probability or impact of it.

Actions for opportunities: Develop

Developing an opportunity is increasing the probability of it occurring. For example, to develop the opportunity of selling your house for more than you have estimated, you might discover that a brand new kitchen is the item that is most attractive to house buyers, and therefore get a new kitchen installed.

Actions for opportunities: Enhance

Enhancing an opportunity increases the impact of it. An illustration of this occurs where there is a chance that a supplier delivers something to you earlier than expected. Enhancing the opportunity would be to ensure you have the capability to use the supplied articles early. Ignoring the opportunity might mean that the new products are stored away unused for a while when they could have been put to good use.

Finally, for each potential action that you have identified, estimate the cost of each action, so that a sensible decision can be made in the next step, 'Select Risk Actions'. The cost of the action is usually the cost of labour to carry out the action plus the cost of any required materials. You may use 'low', 'medium' or 'high' for cost at this point, and you could define ranges for these, e.g., 'low' is £0–£500, 'medium' is £500–£5,000, and 'high' is anything over £5,000.

6.3.4 Select risk actions

The final step of risk analysis is to select which action(s) you are going to use in the project to manage each risk. It is possible to select more than one risk action per risk, for example, you may decide to reduce a threat but then have a contingency plan as well. You need to pick the actions that you believe are the most appropriate given the risk assessment and the cost-effectiveness of each action. Some industries have standards that are applied at this point in the process, e.g., in construction, all threats that are high probability and high impact must be prevented.

6.4 Risk ownership

Monitoring the risks in the Risk Log is a key task. In a large project with many risks, if this monitoring is performed by the Project Manager, then it will take up a large proportion of his time, and may not be performed effectively as the Project Manager is probably not a technical expert in the subject matter of the project. So every risk should be assigned a Risk Owner, who will monitor the risk, check that the risk action is having the desired effect on the risk, and report on the status of the risk to the Project Manager. The Project Manager will use this information to keep the Risk Log up-to-date.

It is sensible for the Risk Owner to be someone who is in a position to monitor the risk closely. For example, in a project that involves the use of a new untested technical tool, the best Owner of the threat that the new tool does not work properly would probably be the technical specialist who will use the tool, rather than the Project Manager. Monitoring of business risks is probably best done by the Project Sponsor rather than the Project Manager. So if there is a threat to the project's Business Case from competition, the Sponsor would usually be in a better position to keep a watch on that risk.

Risk Analysis is now complete. By now the Risk Log is well populated and provides a good baseline for risk management in the project life cycle.

At this point, many Project Managers believe that they have done all they need to in order to manage risks successfully during the rest of the project. A neat, well-formatted Risk Log is now filed away and may not be reviewed again until just before the Project Manager writes the next progress report. A better approach, taken by more proactive Project Managers, is to recognise that the Risk Log needs regular review, perhaps weekly or maybe even daily on a large, complex project.

6.4.1 Manage risks through the project

This consists of two main activities:

- Planning and resourcing the risk actions you have selected
- Monitoring and reporting on the risks and action plans.

Planning and resourcing risk actions

Every risk action that you have decided on needs to be planned, and resources assigned to the action to carry it out. The cost of each action will add cost to your project budget. The risk analysis process has already established that these costs are justified.

For example, a Project Manager who is managing a very technical project may have identified the threat that the project is heavily dependent on one specialist expert in that technical area. The Project Manager might decide to reduce that risk by getting another person trained in that technical area. This will cost money in terms of the price of the training course, the time of the person attending the training course, and perhaps some on-the-job skills transfer from the technical expert to the second person. This is the cost of the action. The cost of all of your risk actions should appear as a line in the project Cost Account (see Chapter 10: Project Controls). In this way, the costs of your risk management activities are visible to the Project Sponsor. The timescale will also be affected, since risk management actions take time to complete. Risk actions should be planned in your Project Plan, just like any other activities in the project.

Monitoring and reporting the risks

Risk Owners will now monitor the risks assigned to them. They should also check the effectiveness of the action plan. This information needs to be reported to the Project Manager regularly so that the Project Manager can keep the Risk Log up-to-date, and also can take action if any of the plans are not effective.

The Project Manager should include an update of the most important risks in the regular progress report sent to the Project Sponsor.

6.5 Risk status

The Risk Log should show the current status of each risk. As part of Project Definition you should decide which different statuses you will use in your project. For example, you could use:

- Current
- Closed
- Decreasing
- Increasing.

During Project Definition the status of all risks identified will be 'current'. As the project progresses the number of current threats should decrease, and hopefully those threats that are not 'closed' should be 'decreasing' in probability or impact. Threats that are 'increasing' in either probability or impact should be re-reviewed and perhaps alternative plans should be made for their management.

6.6 Risk review

The Risk Log is a key document within the Project Management Plan (PMP). The Project Sponsor needs to be kept informed about the overall risk situation for the project. In Chapter 10, Project Controls, the concept of stages within a project is discussed. The Project Sponsor will review the Risk Log at the end of each stage as part of the decision as to whether the project is still viable and therefore whether it should continue. This is part of the ownership of the project by the Project Sponsor, and it helps to develop and maintain stakeholder confidence in the project.

Often it is cheaper and less disruptive to prevent threats from affecting your project's chances of success than it is to fix problems once they have happened. Some opportunities may pass you by unnoticed unless you identify them and try to maximise their chance of occurring and their impact. Project plans will be more accurate, because the estimates for work will take account of the threats in the work. The management of risk means taking a proactive approach to the uncertainty in your project, gives you a greater chance of meeting the project's objectives, and may even bring the organisation more success than was predicted during Project Conception. So Project Managers should be risk-aware, rather than risk-averse.

> "A life spent making mistakes is not only more honourable but more useful than a life spent in doing nothing."
> George Bernard Shaw (Irish playwright)

6.7 Summary

In this chapter you have learnt:

- The benefits of risk management to the Project Manager
- That some risks are opportunities that we don't want to miss

- ➢ How to analyse risks objectively
- ➢ Different ways of managing risks
- ➢ How to incorporate risk actions and contingency plans into your project budget
- ➢ The importance of risk reviews throughout the project.

The next chapter shows you how to manage the delivery of quality in the project. The delivery of poor quality is a major risk for all projects.

6.8 Practical assignment

Produce a Risk Log for the restaurant project. Ensure you have some opportunities as well as threats. For each risk, list the following:

- Description
- Probability
- Impact
- Score (probability x impact)
- Possible Actions
- Cost of Actions
- Selected Action
- Owner.

6.9 Study

Answer the following multiple-choice questions. For answers see Appendix C.

1. Which is the best definition of risk?
   a) Something that might cause the project to fail
   b) Uncertainty in the stakeholders' minds
   c) An event that has occurred and that could be of benefit or detriment to the project
   d) An opportunity to improve project benefits.

2. What is meant by risk assessment?
   a) Evaluating a risk in terms of its likelihood and impact
   b) Checking with the Project Sponsor about the significance of the risk
   c) Deciding a course of action for a risk
   d) Evaluating when the risk might occur.

3. Which of the following is not a valid risk action for a threat?
   a) Transfer
   b) Accept
   c) Ignore
   d) Contingency.

4. When selecting risk actions, which one of the following is most important?
   a) The proximity of the action
   b) The complexity of the action

c) Not having more than one action
d) The cost of the action.

5. A risk that has occurred is…
   a) Something that needs to be notified to the attention of the Project Manager
   b) A risk
   c) Nothing to worry about
   d) Something that should be escalated to the Project Sponsor immediately.

6. How often should risks be reviewed?
   a) Monthly
   b) At the end of each phase of the project
   c) Regularly
   d) Whenever the Sponsor asks for a progress check.

Any one of the six steps above can fail, which can be down to all sorts of reasons: technical misunderstanding, communication difficulties, differences in interpretation. You may well have seen this series of pictures before, but they do emphasise the point effectively:

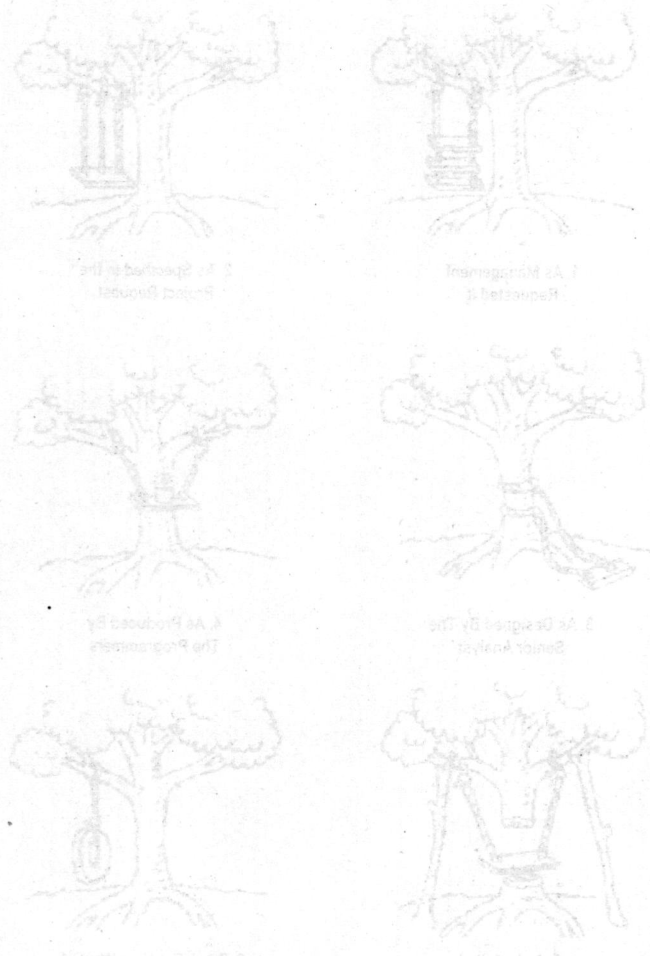

Figure 7.1: What the user wanted.

So we need a clear, unambiguous specification of the customer's requirements that:

- Defines what is to be produced
- Is agreed by both parties
- Can be used to measure the end product against.

Quality applies to all work done by the project, not just the technical products. The management products must also be subject to quality standards.

Quality does not mean 'luxury'. Consider the differences between a designer handbag and a supermarket carrier bag. If all that you know about the customer's requirements

Any one of the six steps above can fail, which can be down to all sorts of reasons: technical misunderstanding, communication difficulties, differences in interpretation. You may well have seen this series of pictures before, but they do emphasise the point effectively:

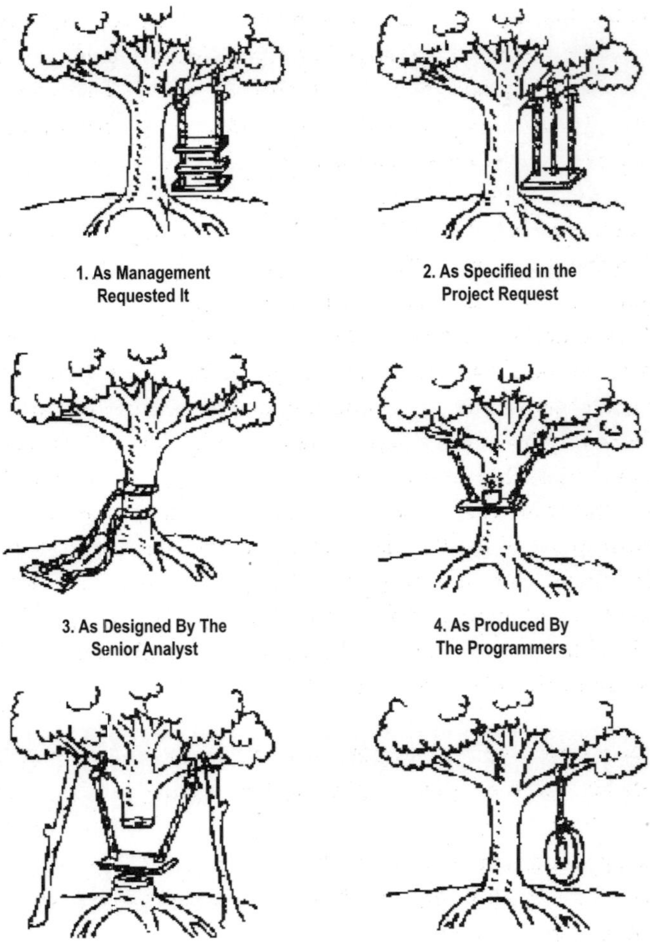

Figure 7.1: What the user wanted.

So we need a clear, unambiguous specification of the customer's requirements that:

- Defines what is to be produced
- Is agreed by both parties
- Can be used to measure the end product against.

Quality applies to all work done by the project, not just the technical products. The management products must also be subject to quality standards.

Quality does not mean 'luxury'. Consider the differences between a designer handbag and a supermarket carrier bag. If all that you know about the customer's requirements is that he needs a lightweight container to carry his shopping, which he can easily fold up and put into his pocket, then a designer handbag is definitely NOT a quality product, and a supermarket carrier bag is.

7.2 Quality Management System

Organisations that run many projects, especially those that have gained accreditation to international quality standards such as ISO:9001, should operate a Quality Management System (QMS), within the context of a Quality Management Policy. This is a set of processes and procedures that is applied to all projects in the organisation. It is effectively the 'manual' that a Project Manager uses to run the project according to the standards agreed by the organisation. It will usually contain things such as standard procedures for managing change requests, templates for documents such as the Business Case, and possibly templates for industry-specific items like design documents.

The QMS defines a consistent way of working for all projects, and therefore all projects can be measured against it to ensure they are following company standards. If an organisation is accredited to any recognised standards, then these will be mentioned in the QMS and the organisation will be subject to regular external audits which it needs to pass in order to retain its certification.

A QMS may alternatively be known as a 'quality system', or 'company manual'. As long as one exists, it is accurate and effective and used consistently by all projects, its name is unimportant.

7.3 Quality Assurance

This is the name of a function within quality management, whose objective is to ensure that the QMS is being used correctly by all projects, is effective and that the projects will meet their objectives. It is also often the name of the team of people (who may be known as 'Quality Managers') who carry out this function. (They may alternatively be known as 'Internal Audit', 'Project Governance' or 'Programme Support'.) Quality Assurance (QA) should be independent of the project teams; it is (usually) a corporate level function.

So QA will perform audits on the organisation's projects. These audits should not be viewed with trepidation by the Project Manager; they are designed to give constructive advice as well as to find errors or inconsistencies. New Project Managers can gain useful insight into the practical application of the QMS by discussions with the company's QA function.

The QA function is also responsible for maintaining the QMS. Based on the lessons learned by all projects, the QA team will update the processes in the QMS to keep them up-to-date, relevant and as efficient as possible. This is one way in which an organisation applies Continuous Process Improvement (CPI).

7.4 Quality Planning

Quality Planning applies at three different levels in a project: Project, Stage and Product.

During Handover and Closeout, Customer Acceptance of the project's products is confirmed, a Lessons Learned report is produced, and acceptance of the products by those who are going to operate and maintain them needs to be obtained. See Chapter 12: Handover and Closeout, for more details.

> "Quality is not an act. It is a habit."
> Aristotle

7.7 Summary

In this chapter you have learnt:

- The definition of quality in a project
- What the quality terms mean
- How to apply the quality terms to a project
- The key quality steps in the project life cycle.

The next chapter shows how to deal with configuration management, which is one of the important aspects of quality. This will help to ensure that you deliver the correct version of each product to the customer, i.e. the one that has been tested against the approved Product Specification and that we can guarantee hasn't been changed since it was last approved.

7.8 Practical assignment

Write a Project Quality Plan for the restaurant project.

7.9 Study

Answer the following multiple-choice questions. For answers see Appendix C.

1. A Quality Management System is best described as:
   a) The strategy for delivering what the customer requires
   b) The planned quality checks in the next stage
   c) ISO 9001
   d) The organisation's standard Project Management procedures.

2. Quality Assurance is:
   a) External auditors visiting the organisation
   b) The activity of providing evidence that quality-related activities are being performed effectively
   c) Producing a Quality Plan
   d) Writing a Lessons Learned Report.

During Handover and Closeout, Customer Acceptance of the project's products is confirmed, a Lessons Learned report is produced, and acceptance of the products by those who are going to operate and maintain them needs to be obtained. See Chapter 12: Handover and Closeout, for more details.

> "Quality is not an act. It is a habit."
> Aristotle.

7.7 Summary

In this chapter you have learnt:

- The definition of quality in a project
- What the quality terms mean
- How to apply the quality terms to a project
- The key quality steps in the project life cycle.

The next chapter shows how to deal with configuration management, which is one of the important aspects of quality. This will help to ensure that you deliver the correct version of each product to the customer, i.e., the one that has been tested against the approved Product Specification, and that we can guarantee hasn't been changed since it was last approved.

7.8 Practical assignment

Write a Project Quality Plan for the restaurant project.

7.9 Study

Answer the following multiple-choice questions. For answers see Appendix C.

1. A Quality Management System is best described as:
   a) The strategy for delivering what the customer requires
   b) The planned quality checks in the next stage
   c) ISO: 9001
   d) The organisation's standard Project Management procedures.

2. Quality Assurance is:
   a) External auditors visiting the organisation
   b) The activity of providing evidence that quality-related activities are being performed effectively
   c) Producing a Quality Plan
   d) Writing a Lessons Learned Report.

3. What is the purpose of a Quality Plan?
   a) To show how quality is to be achieved on a project
   b) To show how quality is to be achieved in an organisation
   c) To audit the quality control work
   d) To ensure that regular quality meetings are held.

4. What is the benefit of maintaining a Quality Log?
   a) It allows blame to be assigned when things go wrong
   b) It provides an audit trail of all quality checking work performed
   c) It allows the Project Manager to estimate the cost of quality
   d) It specifies all of the standards that need to be met.

(continued)

	Product	Version	Status	Location	Owner	Issue No.	Related Products
5.	Room Design	0.1	Draft	Design file	Interior Designer		Project Plan, Requirements Specification, Furniture Order
6.	Furniture Order						Room Design, Installed Furniture
7.	Room Design	0.2	Draft	Design file	Interior Designer	5	Project Plan, Requirements Specification, Furniture Order
8.	Room Design	1.0	Approved	Design file	Interior Designer		Project Plan, Requirements Specification, Furniture Order
9.	Project Plan	1.0	Approved	Project file	Project Manager		Business Case, Risk Log, Room Design
10.	Room Design	2.0	Approved	Design file	Interior Designer	14	Project Plan, Requirements Specification, Furniture Order

The sample rows of data in this table have been created by the project events as follows:

Row	Event
1.	The Business Case was drafted. It is held in the Project file and owned by the Project Sponsor. If it changes, the Project Plan and Risk Log may need to be changed, or if they change, the Business Case may need to change.
2.	The Business Case was approved.
3.	The Project Plan was drafted. Again, any changes to this will impact the Business Case and Risk Log, and vice versa.
4.	The Requirements Specification was approved. This will be used in the development of the Room Design.
5.	The Room Design was drafted.
6.	The Furniture Order was identified as a product that needs to be tracked, but work has not yet started on this product.
7.	The Room Design was re-drafted and is now at version 1.0. The reason for this re-draft can be found in Issue No. 5 in the project Issue Log.
8.	The Room Design has passed its quality check and is now approved.

(continued)

(continued)

Row	Event
9.	The Project Plan has now been updated in accordance with the approved Room Design, and approved.
10.	The Room Design was changed due to Issue No. 14, is now at version 2.0, and has been approved at this new version.

Configuration management gives the Project Manager control of all the different elements of the project: physical things, software, documents or drawings. So the database above contains information about the Business Case and Project Plan, which are management products, as well as the technical products such as the Room Design and Furniture Order. It is more difficult to control physical items such as a carpet or a painted wall, but the project may build different versions of them during the project life cycle; for example, you may build a prototype of a machine or a model of a new building. It is still important to know which versions of these items have been subject to formal approvals, and which change requests have been applied to these items.

The only products that will not be managed this way are the logs such as the Issue Log. You would not expect to add a row to the configuration database every time a new Issue is added to the Issue Log. This would be duplication of information.

Using this database, the history of any product can be viewed. Also, the current version of any item can always be found; this avoids the risk of working on items that have been superseded by later versions.

"The next best thing to knowing something is knowing where to find it."
Samuel Johnson (18th century English literary figure)

8.1 Functions of configuration management

There are five activities involved in configuration management:

1. **Identify the configuration items.** This means giving each product a unique reference. For technical products, this step is related to the WBS (Work Breakdown Structure), as usually each task in a project leads to a product. Management products should also be identified, but this is usually a fairly simple task as they are common to most projects.
2. **Plan the strategy** for configuration management by producing a Configuration Management Plan. This will be part of the Project Management Plan (PMP) and should contain the following headings:

   - **How the configuration will be managed**
     This will refer to any method or tool to be used. On large IT projects, it is common to use a configuration management software tool. On small projects, a simple table which is manually updated will normally be adequate.

- The contents of a Configuration Management Plan
- The relationship between configuration management and change control.

The next chapter shows how to deal with controlling change, another important aspect of quality. Change control and configuration management work closely together to ensure that the correct versions of products are controlled and delivered.

8.3 Practical assignment

Produce a Configuration Management Plan for the restaurant project.

8.4 Study

Answer the following multiple-choice questions. For answers see Appendix C.

1. The configuration of a project is best described as:
   a) The latest version number of all products
   b) The total of all the management products
   c) The sum total of all products in the project
   d) The sum total of all technical products.

2. Project assets are:
   a) The resources
   b) The teams
   c) The Project Manager and the Project Sponsor
   d) The products.

3. How is the configuration database related to the Work Breakdown Structure?
   a) Each task in the WBS usually leads to a configuration item
   b) The WBS shows each version of a product
   c) The configuration database shows the order in which products are developed
   d) The Configuration Librarian maintains both.

4. Who is responsible for ensuring that configuration management is successfully implemented?
   a) Project Manager
   b) Project Sponsor
   c) Configuration Manager
   d) Configuration Librarian.

- ➢ The contents of a Configuration Management Plan
- ➢ The relationship between configuration management and change control.

The next chapter shows how to deal with controlling change, another important aspect of quality. Change control and configuration management work closely together to ensure that the correct versions of products are controlled and delivered.

8.3 Practical assignment

Produce a Configuration Management Plan for the restaurant project.

8.4 Study

Answer the following multiple-choice questions. For answers see Appendix C.

1. The configuration of a project is best described as:
   a) The latest version number of all products
   b) The total of all the management products
   c) The sum total of all products in the project
   d) The sum total of all technical products.

2. Project assets are:
   a) The resources
   b) The teams
   c) The Project Manager and the Project Sponsor
   d) The products.

3. How is the configuration database related to the Work Breakdown Structure?
   a) Each task in the WBS usually leads to a configuration item
   b) The WBS shows each version of a product
   c) The configuration database shows the order in which products are developed
   d) The Configuration Librarian maintains both.

4. Who is responsible for ensuring that configuration management is successfully implemented?
   a) Project Manager
   b) Project Sponsor
   c) Configuration Manager
   d) Configuration Librarian.

The project manager's diary

Planning out the strategy for configuration management gave me a few headaches as the fact that we didn't have Project Support meant that I had to accept the jobs of configuration control and status accounting. I'll be going into the database and changing the product statuses from 'draft' to 'approved'. It's a bit tedious but it has to be done. This is, I guess, what I'll be doing in my evenings when everyone else has gone home. Why is it that, in so many organisations, Project Managers are expected to not have a life?

Working out how we would do configuration management (spreadsheet; we don't need a software package to do this on this relatively simple project) and sorting out the filing structure and security were pretty easy. Again we hit the problem of the Project Board and Project Assurance. In this case, they are responsible for auditing the configuration management system to maintain its accuracy. I stuck to my guns and listed them as responsible but I can see now that I'll be doing that. I can't see the new restaurant manager wanting to spot-check the database, I'm sure he'll see this as below him.

But I'll make sure it gets done properly, as otherwise I'll have sleepless nights about the loss of key documents or someone over-writing approved technical specifications.

9 Change management: Controlling project change

This chapter outlines the importance of managing change in a controlled manner throughout a project. It suggests a process for change control, and suggests which elements should be considered when assessing the impact of proposed changes.

Project Managers are arbiters of change. All projects implement change to the users of the end product. But the project itself will be subject to change throughout its life cycle. A good Project Manager will accept that some change is inevitable, but will seek to manage those changes carefully.

9.1 What is a change?

Changes in a project can arise from:

- Changes in customer requirements
- Changes to the scope of the project
- Changes to the specification of a product
- Mistakes
- Errors in estimating
- Key resources being taken away to higher-priority projects
- Changes in organisational strategy
- The realisation that the original plan was too ambitious
- Discovery of a task dependency that wasn't spotted beforehand
- ... and so on.

"All things are in a state of flux."
Heraclites (Greek philosopher)

For many of the sources of change above, the change may originate as a project Issue. An Issue is a problem that will impact on the project objectives if it is not resolved. When an Issue is raised, the originator of the Issue may not always be aware that resolution of the Issue will require changes to be made. The Project Manager will analyse Issues to determine how they are to be resolved. Some Issues may not lead to a change. For example, if you are building a house, your garden designer may be waiting for you to decide how much lawn area you require in the garden. If they haven't started the garden design yet, then this will not be a change, but they may raise it as an Issue because if you don't make the decision soon then the project timescales will be affected. Other Issues that may lead to changes are things like differences in interpretation of requirements, and items missed out of the project definition which are realised later on.

Changes can originate from many different sources, and the resulting management of the change can mean changes to:

- The Project Management Plan (PMP)
- The Business Case
- The Project Plan
- A Stage Plan
- A task
- A technical product (which may already have been approved)
- Any other management or specialist product.

Formal change control will help to avoid 'scope creep' by using a recognised procedure for managing changes. This will ensure that the changes that are implemented are the ones that will give some benefit to the project or the business. It will ensure that any increases in time or cost as a result of changes are understood, visible and accounted for, which in turn will limit the risk of project failure or failure to meet the Business Case. Formal change control will ensure that the Project Plan and Stage Plans are kept up-to-date throughout the project life cycle.

9.2 Change control process

Figure 9.1 below shows a sensible process for change control:

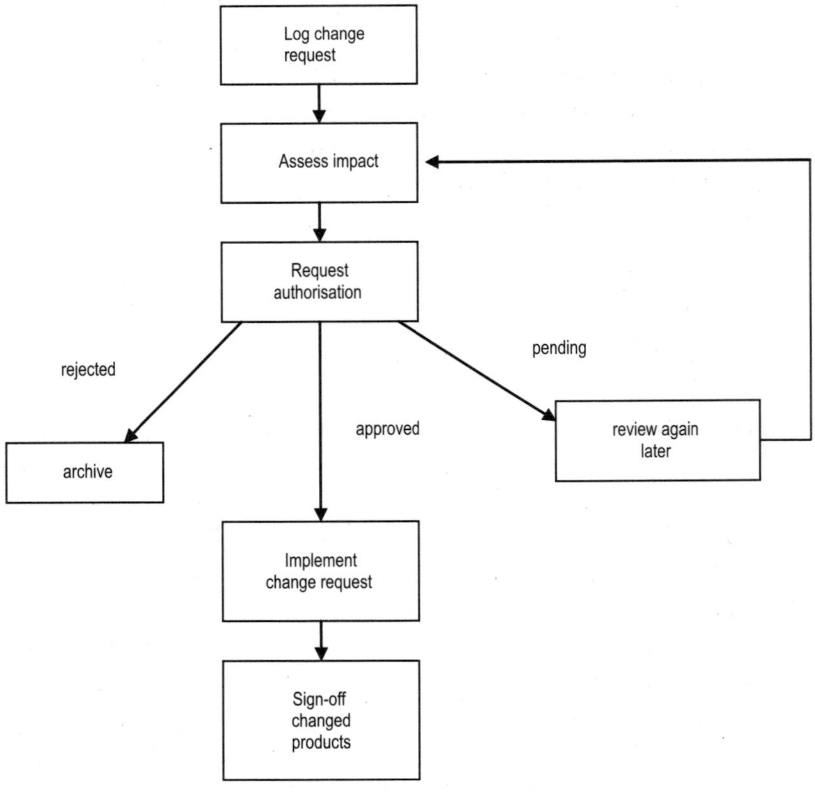

Figure 9.1: A change control process.

Each change request should be logged so that:

- The Project Manager always knows how many change requests are outstanding
- The current project scope is always defined
- The customer is clear about the end products they will receive
- The PMP reflects the current position of the project definition, scope, requirements, activities, resources, cost, time and so on
- All changes are communicated to key stakeholders.

This means that even changes that require no extra effort or have no cost implication need to be processed formally. For example, before a website page is developed, the colour scheme may be changed. This won't cost any more money or require any more effort, but the documented specification must be accurate. A Change Request could even save some project cost, but this would still need to be communicated.

The Change Log should, as a minimum, contain the following:

- Change Request No
- Originator
- Description
- Impact assessment
- Decision
- Status.

The impact of each change request should be assessed. This should cover:

- What needs to be changed (i.e., which products will need to be changed, and which other products will therefore need to be changed. To obtain this information you should look at the 'related products' field within the configuration database).
- What is the justification or pressure for the change? Will it achieve a cost saving, or an increase in project benefits, or is it the result of an Issue that needs resolving?
- How will the change impact on the timescale?
- What will the change cost?
- Will the change impact on performance or quality?
- Will the change impact on the business benefits?
- Will the change impact on risks?
- Do we have the resources to make the change?

Once the impact of the change is fully understood, authorisation to make the change should be requested from the project Change Authority. This will usually be the Project Sponsor, or may be a responsibility undertaken jointly by the Project Board. On large projects, the Project Sponsor/Board may not wish to be involved in the approval of all change requests, so they may delegate this authority to another person or group. The Change Authority may be assigned an allowance, which is to be spent on implementing approved changes; this is known as a Change Budget, and it is commonly used when there is an expectation of a fair amount of changes being requested from the users. For example, if the requirements are known to be sketchy or you suspect that not all of the users were involved in specifying them, you may decide it is realistic to set aside some money for changes.

If the Change Authority approves the change, then usually the work to carry out the change will start. The change may be rejected, in which case the change request details need to be retained on file. Or it may be decided to 'hold' the change request for now and return to it later when we will have a better idea of whether we have enough time and money left in the budget.

If the change request is to be implemented, then the Project Manager needs to ensure that all technical products affected by the change are updated and tested. All management products also need to be updated and approved. (In particular, the Project Plan will show the new cost and time of the project.) So there will be a number of new rows in the configuration database as new versions of these products are created. This may also mean changes to contracts, if the change affects external suppliers.

At all points during this process, the Change Log should be kept up-to-date.

9.3 Summary

In this chapter you have learnt:

- The importance of managing project change
- A change control process
- How to analyse the impact of a proposed change
- The relationship between changes and Issues
- The importance of keeping a log of all project changes.

This chapter has dealt with the control of changes in a project. The next chapter covers the entire topic of control for a project, making sure that once the PMP is approved and work starts, the Project Manager and the rest of the project organisation carry out the monitoring and control of all project elements, to keep the project on track or to take remedial action if it starts to deviate from the plan.

9.4 Practical assignment

Imagine that the restaurant project is currently at 19 February in the Project Plan in Appendix B. The project is exactly on schedule so far. The Project Sponsor has just suggested that the restaurant is altered from an Asian-style one to an American diner. Carry out an impact analysis on the change request.

9.5 Study

Answer the following multiple-choice questions. For answers see Appendix C.

1. Who approves Change Requests?
   a) The Project Manager
   b) Project Assurance

c) The user representative on the Project Board
d) The Change Authority.

2. A change request may refer to:
   a) A change to a product specification
   b) A change to the location of the project team
   c) An increase or decrease in project scope
   d) All of the above, and more.

3. How is Configuration Management related to Change Control?
   a) All changes to products result in a new version, which is logged in the configuration database
   b) It isn't related
   c) The Change Log is managed under Configuration Management
   d) Both are the responsibility of the Project Support role.

4. Which of the following is false about Change Control?
   a) The Change Log is a database of all changes requested on the project
   b) The Project Manager does not approve change requests
   c) Changes that do not cost money need no formal management
   d) A lack of change control may result in scope creep.

The project manager's diary

I had a bit of a job trying to persuade Charlie of the need for a change control process. This is quite typical really as I guess most of the changes would probably come from him, as he walks round the half-built site or tastes a new menu idea in the kitchen. I guess he realises this and wants to be able to change anything he fancies but doesn't want me coming back and saying that it will cost him more or take us longer to make the changes.

I asked him how he would feel if, whilst walking round the site, he decided he wanted to change the plain wallpaper to some fancy silk. Custom silk is expensive and takes ages to obtain, so this would delay the rest of the project and also increase costs. If we just went ahead with that change and didn't analyse its impact properly, and this meant a costly knock-on effect in terms of changes to the other branded items such as the launch invitations, advertisements and menu designs, then this would have the potential to allow the costs to creep up unnoticed. I think this attention to his wallet focused his mind somewhat and he agreed that he needed to sign off all changes.

After this he was also quite keen to limit the cost of changes as much as possible. So we agreed a change budget of £8K. This meant I had to update the Cost Account and Business Case to show the new total project cost, and I updated the Change Request form so that for each change it would show how much of the £8K was left at that time.

10 Controls: Keeping the project on track

Once the Project Management Plan (PMP) is written and approved, it is not enough to hope that everything goes according to the plan. The Project Manager needs to monitor the plans, control the work and keep the plans up-to-date throughout the Implementation phase of the project. This chapter outlines the different controls that are needed to ensure that the project remains on track, or that deviations are spotted early for immediate remedial action. It also lists sets of daily, weekly and monthly tasks that it is suggested a Project Manager carries out in order to ensure that nothing is forgotten.

10.1 Stages

How do you eat an elephant? One bite at a time. Similarly, a project should be broken down into stages. This is not a reference to the project phases (Conception, Definition, Implementation and Handover and Closeout), nor is it a reference to the technical stages (e.g., Requirements, Design, Build, Test etc.). 'Stages' are more accurately known as 'management stages' because they are chunks of the project separated by decision points, where the Project Board will undertake a management review of the project and decide whether it should continue. There is some overlap between the project phases and management stages, because (as we have already seen) the Project Board will approve progress into Definition based on the Business Case and Definition Phase Plan, and progress into Implementation based on the PMP. But really management stages are the division of the Implementation phase into sections so that:

- We can make the decision about the on-going viability of the project at suitable points
- We can plan in detail one stage at a time and hence use the benefit of hindsight when we write the next Stage Plan
- We can exercise the appropriate levels of control over the work in one stage at a time
- We take time to step backwards from the project and review the project approach to quality, communication, change control, and so on.

There is no formula for deciding where your stages should be. Instead, you need to take into account sensible points for the Project Board to make its viability decisions, how far ahead you are able to plan the project in detail, and how much control the Project Board requires over the project (the more stage boundaries, the more control they have). Sometimes stage boundaries are known as 'gate reviews' or 'go/no go' decision points.

Using the example of a project to decorate a room that we used in Chapter 3: Planning, we could consider applying stage boundaries to the Gantt chart below:

ID	Task Name	Duration
1	**1 Design**	**3 days**
2	**4 Prepare Room**	**3 days**
3	**2 Painting**	**7 days**
4	2.1 Buy Paint	1 day
5	2.2 Paint Walls & Ceiling	2 days
6	2.3 Paint Woodwork	2 days
7	**3 Lay Carpet**	**1 day**
8	**5 Furnish**	**9 days**
9	5.1 Order Furniture	1 day
10	5.3 Await Furniture Delivery	1 day
11	5.2 Install Furniture	1 day

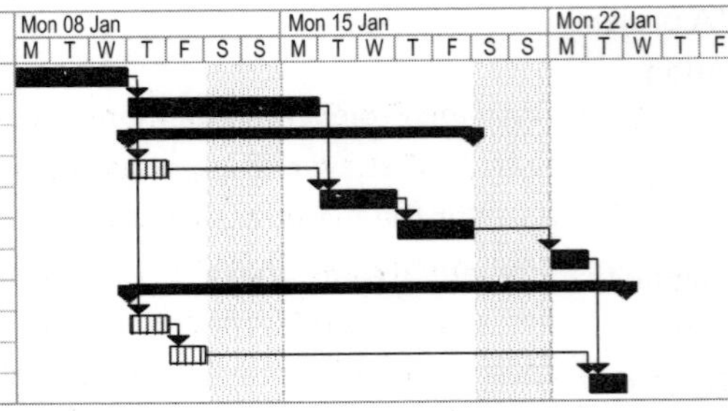

Figure 10.1: Microsoft project Gantt chart for decorating a room.

The first stage will start on Mon 8 Jan and end on Wed 10 Jan

It would be sensible to have a management review of the project after the design has been completed, as this may have changed the estimates for the project cost and time, and hence affect the Business Case. The Project Board will welcome the opportunity to review the viability of the project. Also, we are about to buy the paint and order the furniture, so before these financial commitments are made, it would be a good idea to review our commitment to the project.

The second stage will start on Thurs 11 Jan and end on Mon 15 Jan

This will allow the Project Board to check the viability of the project whilst the critical activities are executed. If the project is running late then it could, for example, choose to employ another painter so that the woodwork could be done in parallel with the walls and ceiling. Equally, this second stage could have ended on Wed 17 Jan (after completion of the walls and ceiling) or Fri 19 Jan (after completion of the woodwork). The positioning of this stage boundary depends on the preferences of the Project Board.

The third stage will start on Tues 16 Jan and end on Fri 19 Jan

All the paintwork should have been completed, but this will give the Project Board the opportunity to check that it is entirely satisfied with the paintwork before the carpet is laid. Once the carpet is laid, it is a much more risky task to improve the paintwork!

The last stage will start on Monday 22 Jan and end on Tuesday 23 Jan

Clearly the last stage boundary, at the end of Tuesday 23 Jan, is not concerned with the on-going viability of the project. But this will give the Project Board the chance to accept the final products and give the Project Manager approval to continue into the Handover and Closeout phase.

Clearly this is a very small project but the concept of management stages is scalable to any size of project. On a larger project, such as a complex IT system, often the control points revolve around major deliverables such as the prototype, design, build and integration testing having been completed. In construction projects, stage boundaries tend to occur at major events such as getting planning approval and receipt of tenders.

Stage boundaries should be shown on the Project Plan in the PMP.

> "A project gets a year late one day at a time."
> Anon

10.2 Tolerance

Imagine that you are a Project Manager managing a stage with a budget of £100K and a timescale of 100 days. The stage has just started, but already some small Issues have occurred and you are now predicting that the stage will cost £101K and take 101 days. Should you escalate this to the Project Board? Most people would answer 'no' because the Project Board is a group of busy people who trust you to make the right decisions. But what should you do if, a little later on, more Issues have occurred and you are now predicting a cost of £120K and a time of 120 days? Most people would say that clearly the Project Manager has to involve the Project Board.

So where do we draw the line between handling a problem ourselves, and escalating it upwards? The answer lies in the use of Tolerance. Tolerance is the amount of deviation a plan is allowed before the Project Manager has to escalate the problem to the Project Board. It is normally specified in terms of a percentage on the budgets for planned time and cost. For example, the Project Board might specify a tolerance of 10% on cost, and 5% on time, if the project is more time-critical than cost-critical. Then the decision as to whether the problem needs escalating is a mathematical one, rather than a political one.

This helps to remove some stress from the Project Manager who has been worrying about whether to tell the Project Board about an Issue. Murphy's Law states that if the Project Manager tells the Project Board, the Project Board will be irritated by the apparent trivial nature of the Issues and respond with 'we are paying you to manage this', and if the Project Manager doesn't tell the Project Board, it will get quite angry roof when it finally finds out about the Issue and wonder (very loudly) why the Project Manager didn't report it. Tolerance goes a long way to removing this communication problem from the project.

Tolerance can also be specified on the scope or quality of the project. This allows some flexibility when time and money tolerances have been spent. Scope tolerance allows the customer to specify which elements of the project are 'mandatory', and which are only 'desirable'. For example, for your budget you may require a four bedroom house but you may be relaxed about whether or not you have a study. Quality tolerance does not alter whether or not some items are delivered, but instead allows some movement on the specification of certain elements. For example, you might specify that the kitchen floor of your new house should be made from maple, but you might allow any kind of real wood as long as laminated flooring is not used.

Tolerances should be documented in the Project Plan in the PMP, and in individual Stage Plans. Stage tolerances will normally be assigned when the Project Board approve the Stage Plan at the stage boundary.

10.3 Reporting

Progress reports are a communication mechanism that act as a control because they inform the recipient about the current progress, amount spent so far against the cost and time budgets, and plans for the next reporting period. They provide a regular discipline for the Project Manager in gathering the information. They should be seen as status reports, not ways of raising problems or questions; if they are used to raise things that need a response, the response may be delayed because the recipient of a progress report does not always read it straight away. The progress reports that a Project Manager prepares for the Project Board should give an accurate snapshot of the current situation, enabling the Project Board either to feel confident in the progress within the stage so far, or to ask searching questions about the information provided in order to uncover any potential problems.

Progress reports usually report the current status of progress against KPIs (Key Performance Indicators). These are measures of how well the project is moving towards meeting its success criteria (these were discussed in Chapter 5: Stakeholder Management). A simple example of a KPI is based on cost and time; by this point in the project the planned spend is compared against the actual spend. Other KPIs can be based on reaching milestones, such as having designs or specifications approved, or having carried out a certain number of quality checks. Combined together, KPIs are a useful indication of the health of the project. They should be documented in the PMP and therefore approved before work starts.

Typical progress report contents are:

- Date
- Period covered by the report
- Money spent this period
- Work done this period
- Stage time tolerance left
- Stage cost tolerance left
- Update on key risks
- Planned work for the next period
- Progress against any other KPIs.

Progress reports should be listed in the Communication Plan in the PMP. This enables the Project Board to agree the frequency, method of delivery and content of the reports before the project moves into the Implementation phase.

10.4 Progress meetings

One of the decisions that needs to be made about how the project will be controlled concerns the use of progress meetings. It is quite usual for the Project Manager to have regular (often weekly) meetings with the Team Managers, as a close working relationship needs to be developed, especially if the supplier is external. But whether or not the Project Manager needs to have regular meetings with the Project Board is a more tricky decision. The advantages of having regular meetings are:

- The Project Manager sees the Project Board on a regular basis
- Project communication and a feeling of team identity can be enhanced
- Body language of attendees is more effective in communication than relying only on the written word.

But the disadvantages are:

- The potential for a large waste of time when there was no real need for a meeting
- The temptation of the Project Board to wait until the meeting to read the Project Manager's progress report
- Attendees can bring along their own 'hidden agendas'
- Attendees can be unwilling to speak the truth in a formal situation.

In most organisations, the Project Manager has regular, monthly progress meetings with the Project Board. To maintain their effectiveness, the key thing is to take note of the disadvantages and ensure that they don't apply to your project. Meetings should be organised properly around an agenda, which is circulated well in advance, run effectively and diplomatically by a capable chairman, resulting in a concise summary of actions produced by Project Support. Care needs to be taken to ensure that the minutes provide an accurate record of the actions and decisions made; it is easy to unintentionally introduce bias. The actions should be completed in good time after the meeting by the attendees.

Meetings should be documented in the Communication Plan in the PMP, so that the strategy for them can be approved by the Project Board.

10.5 Cost Account

The Cost Account is a spreadsheet which assists the control of costs throughout the project.

Based on the following Cost Breakdown Structure for Decorating a Room, a project in Chapter 3, the Cost Account lists items in a tabular form, and also accounts for the costs of Project Management, risk mitigation and changes.

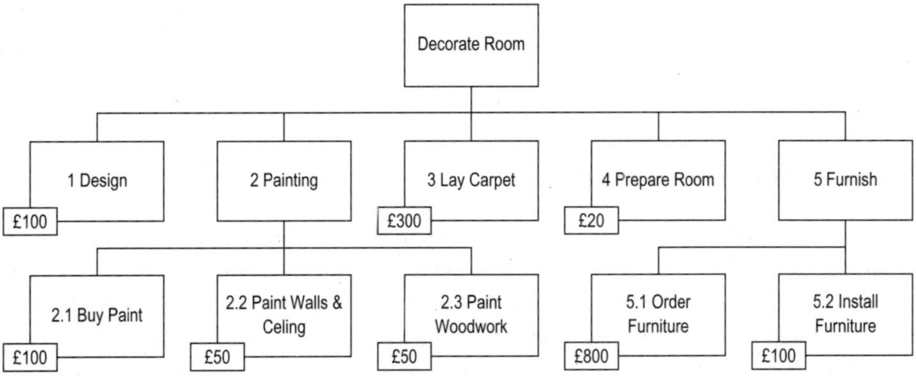

Figure 10.2: Cost Breakdown Structure.

		Estimates			Actuals		
Item ref.	**Item**	**Labour Cost**	**Materials Cost**	**Total Cost**	**Labour Cost**	**Materials Cost**	**Total Cost**
1	Design	100		100			
2.1	Buy paint		100	100			
2.2	Paint walls and ceiling	50		50			
2.3	Paint woodwork	50		50			
3	Lay carpet	100	200	300			
4	Prepare room	20		20			
5.1	Order furniture		800	800			
5.2	Install furniture	100		100			
	Project Management			750			
	Total planned work			**2,270**			
	Contingency budget			200			
	Change budget			500			
	Total allowed budget			**2,970**			

Figure 10.3: Cost Account.

The Cost Account lists the estimated labour and materials cost for each element of the Cost Breakdown Structure. Project Management will last for the duration of the project, in this case 15 days. The Project Manager is part-time on this project so he is costing the project management at only £50 per day. So the Planned Work on the project is £2,270. But to be realistic, the Cost Account needs to show allowances; amounts of money set aside against particular things. The Change budget is a measure of how much we believe the users will change their minds about their requirements, and how much this may cost. The Contingency budget is money set aside against certain risks on the Risk Log, for which we have contingency actions planned. In the perfect world, neither of these allowances would be spent, because the users won't change their minds and the risks won't occur.

The Cost Account will be part of the Project Plan and should be updated with actual values as the project progresses. It is sensible to attach the Cost Account to the progress report.

10.6 Issue management

Issues are unexpected events, problems, ideas, queries; in fact anything that needs to be drawn to the attention of the Project Manager. It is important that anyone can raise an Issue, so that all comments, queries and problems are processed properly. So the Project Manager should set out in the PMP the method for raising Issues.

One of the functions of the Project Support role is to log Issues in the Issue Log. Then the Project Manager will inspect each Issue to see what sort of Issue it is and what the likely impact will be. If the Issue causes the Project Manager to forecast that this will take the current stage outside tolerance in either time or cost, then the Issue should be escalated to the Project Board. If the Issue is less serious, then the Project Manager should deal with it himself.

Whatever the outcome of the Issue, the Issue Log should be kept up-to-date so that it provides an audit trail of project events.

The APM (Association for Project Management) definition of an Issue is more specific; it defines an Issue as something that the Project Manager cannot resolve, and therefore has to be escalated to the Project Sponsor. It is not crucial to project success what the actual names of these events are; what is more important is that there is clear definition and understanding of what happens to these unexpected events, who is responsible for dealing with them, and that they are all tracked. The strategy for handling these events should be clearly documented in the PMP and hence it will be approved by the Project Sponsor.

10.7 Checklists

The following are designed to be used as checklists by the Project Manager to ensure that all Project Management processes are working smoothly and all documentation is kept up-to-date. If the Project Manager operates an electronic diary, then these items can be set as reminders.

10.7.1 Daily Project Manager tasks

1. Check Issue Log and assess new Issues immediately:
    - Add any new Risks to Risk Log including risk analysis and planned risk management actions
    - Add new Change Requests to Change Log and arrange for them to be assessed
    - Escalate any Issue which will take the stage or project outside tolerance, or anything which the Project Board should be made aware of.
2. If there are any increases in cost/time, update the current Stage Plan.
3. Keep the teams busy by issuing new work when the previous task is complete.
4. Manage By Walk About (MBWA). This is an important part of managing the individuals in the project. Project Managers should not 'hide' behind their computer screens or office doors; they should maintain face-to-face relationships with everyone in the project.

10.7.2 Weekly Project Manager tasks

1. Hold a progress meeting with each Team Manager.
2. Update current Stage Plan: put progress figures into the Gantt Chart and Cost Account.
3. Update Project Plan: put progress figures into the Gantt Chart, Cost Account.
4. Review the Risk Log and update with information from Risk Owners; escalate any major risks.
5. Check on progress of Change Requests and update the Change Log.

6. Review the Quality Log to check the progress of the teams.
7. Ensure communication is maintained as specified in the Communication Plan.
8. Liaise with Project Assurance.

10.7.3 Monthly Project Manager tasks

1. Carry out an informal review of the project (Project Evaluation Review).
2. Send a progress report to Project Board.
3. Hold a progress meeting with the Project Board, if you have decided that they are to be a project control.
4. Verify the Configuration Management database.
5. Talk to key stakeholders to assess their current position and update your Stakeholder Analysis.
6. Note down any lessons learned.
7. Check the progress of the current stage to see when the next stage should be planned.
8. Consider opportunities for team-building.
9. Attend some of the quality checks.

10.8 How Project Management topics relate

Project Management topics are linked to each other by a set of connections. For example, risk is related to planning because when new risks are found, the management actions to mitigate those risks should be added to the plans. Once a plan is written, the risky areas of the plan, such as the critical path, will be visible, and this will lead to new risks being identified.

To express those links in a visual form, the following diagram summarises how the management products relate to each other:

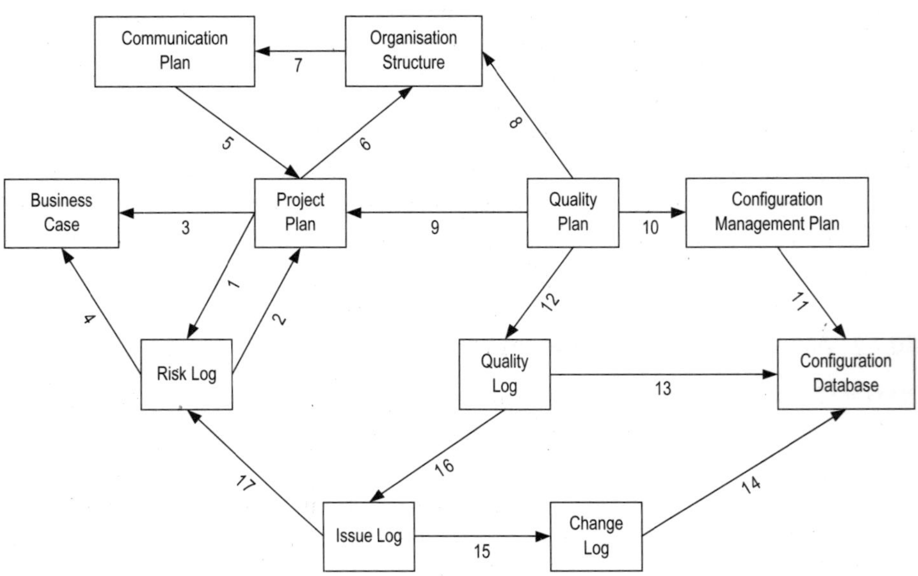

Figure 10.4: Relationships between Project Management products.

Item	Relationship
1.	The Project Plan will identify risks to be added to the Risk Log.
2.	The risk actions should be planned, resourced and costed in the Project Plan.
3.	The Project Plan derives the cost and time, which are held in the Business Case.
4.	Major risks are summarised in the Business Case.
5.	Communication actions should be planned, resourced and costed in the Project Plan.
6.	The Project Plan will determine the resources required, to be shown in the Organisation Structure.
7.	The Communication Plan will ensure everyone in the Organisation Structure is kept informed.
8.	The Quality Plan will impose quality responsibilities on project roles.
9.	Quality work should be planned, resourced and costed in the Project Plan.
10.	The Quality Plan should incorporate the Configuration Management Plan.
11.	The Configuration Management Plan determines the structure of the configuration database.
12.	The Quality Plan determines the quality checking strategy, which is used to produce the Quality Log.
13.	Product approval via quality checking causes an update to the configuration database.
14.	Changes will create a new record in the configuration database.
15.	Project Issues may be Changes, once they have been assessed.
16.	Unresolved quality checking errors may become Issues.
17.	Project Issues may become Risks.

This diagram will be useful for the Project Manager during the Implementation phase to ensure that information is correctly stored and updated.

> "Projects undertaken using a proven method carry less risk and a greater chance of success than unstructured projects."
> Gartner Group April 1999

10.9 Summary

In this chapter you have learnt:

- Stages are an important control for the Project Board to check project viability
- Tolerance is a useful way to specify when Issues need to be escalated
- The Cost Account helps to control project costs
- All of the management products are inter-related.

The next chapter covers management of the most important resources in the project, but which you cannot manage using a procedure: people.

10.10 Practical assignment

Using the sample solution in Appendix B, decide where the stage boundaries should be and produce a Cost Account for the restaurant project.

10.11 Study

Answer the following multiple-choice questions. For answers see Appendix C.

1. Which of these is the most important factor in deciding where stage boundaries should be?
   a) When meetings are scheduled
   b) How many people are on the Project Board
   c) How many tasks are about to start
   d) The commitment of people and money to the next stage.

2. Which of these statements is true?
   a) Tolerance is the allowed overrun, which doesn't need escalation
   b) Progress meetings are always necessary
   c) Tolerance allows the Project Manager to do whatever he likes
   d) Stage boundaries are at regular intervals.

3. Name two allowances normally found in the Cost Account
   a) Tolerance
   b) Risk mitigation
   c) Issue management
   d) Change Budget and Contingency Budget.

4. Which of the following should appear in a Progress Report?
   a) A new risk
   b) A query that the Project Manager needs resolving by the Project Sponsor
   c) Update on time and money spent so far
   d) Details of staff appraisal discussions.

The project manager's diary

Sorting out the project controls was the last part of the PMP so I was now feeling quite happy about what I'd produced so far. The Definition phase was nearly at an end and although it was still within time and cost budgets, I had to use all of my assertiveness skills in order to press forward and get things defined properly. I could see that Charlie was getting quite jumpy about getting on with the Implementation phase as he wanted to see some tangible results after all this management work. Today he asked me whether or not the contractors had been appointed; I had to remind him that he hadn't signed off the PMP yet.

We worked on the allocation of stage boundaries on the Project Plan. I put together some suggestions for Charlie's approval. The third stage boundary is clearly crucial but we had some issues surrounding his availability due to some golf tournament in Scotland, but I'm not too worried. The timing of stage boundaries to be exactly when one set of tasks has been completed and before any tasks in the next set have been started is almost impossible. Practically, you have to have the management review just before something has quite finished, or get on with the next stage without approval for a couple of days or so. As long as the Project Board understands this then we all know where we are.

Charlie and I agreed that I would send him a progress report each Friday afternoon and we agreed the headings I would cover. All of this is standard apart from a couple of things he added. He wants me to keep him updated weekly on the identification of celebrities to attend the launch event, and he wanted me to comment on the staff we had recruited and how they were settling in and getting on together. He knows that restaurants are high-pressured environments! I told him that a better communication method for the latter point was verbal, rather than documenting my opinions about people.

So, finally the PMP is complete!

As I had been discussing its contents with Charlie throughout Definition, nothing in the document surprised him and he signed it off without any comment. He doesn't yet have a Supplier Rep to support him as we haven't engaged the building firm. The User Rep will be the new Restaurant Manager, Nick Noodle.

So then we started the Implementation phase.

The first stage boundary raised some interesting things—Charlie didn't really understand the importance of the management review. His view was that as the project had started, of course it was going to continue. I explained that the review was not solely about the viability of the project, but a chance for the Project Board to review other things they had to monitor, such as the achievement of quality so far, the strategies for communication, stakeholder management, and the management of risk. We needed to discuss the issue of what was going to happen on 12 February when five new people join the project—is he going to be around to help with me that?

What frustrated me was that Charlie had not read any of my progress reports or my summary of the stage just completed. I had to sit in the meeting while he read them through. He obviously feels that as long as I'm writing them, he knows that I am collating the facts and figures correctly. I guess at some level he is right—if there were any major Issues then I would raise them separately to ensure that they were acted upon immediately. But he needs to be taking more ownership, and it's a waste of my time to be sitting there quietly when I could be sorting out the Issues with the Architect.

11 People management: Getting the best from your team

People are unpredictable beings who cannot all be managed in the same way. This chapter outlines some of the people management skills that the Project Manager needs to use in order to manage the team to deliver a successful project conclusion. Interpersonal skills such as communication and negotiation are required in many different Project Management situations. Basic models to help with understanding motivation, leadership and team-building are explained. There are many sources of further information you could seek which would be relevant here, for example, you might wish to read about wider topics such as body language.

11.1 Communication

Communication is crucial to successful Project Management. The Project Manager is constantly communicating with many different people at different levels and about many different topics. Poor communication is seen by many Project Managers as one of the major reasons for project failure.

Communication is a two-way process. We transmit a message and this gets interpreted by the recipient. If we do not check their understanding, then we do not know if what we said was interpreted correctly. Good communication relies on active listening by the recipient; the ability to listen carefully without waiting for the other person to draw breath (so that there is a chance to interrupt), reflecting back the message that has been received to check understanding, and showing (rather than feigning) interest in the message by the use of appropriate body language.

There are many different communication media, each with its advantages and disadvantages. It is important to pick the appropriate medium for the message. Examples of inappropriate choices of medium include:

- Sending confidential information via email
- Trying to resolve a personality clash between two people in a public meeting
- Explaining complex technical theories via telephone
- Sending an email to 'everyone' rather than risk missing someone out
- Sacking your staff via text message.

It is worth noting that when a message is verbally transmitted in person, the amount of the message that is picked up by the receiver is in the following proportions:

- 7% is down to the words
- 38% is down to the tone of voice
- 55% is down to the body language.

This means that email, on which we rely so heavily these days, 'leaves out' most of the message. This is why you may receive an email and be unsure as to whether the sender is being sarcastic, humorous or just critical. At least if they telephoned you, you would be able to deduce a lot more from the tone of their voice. The communication would be even clearer if they came and met you face-to-face.

> "The most important thing in communication is hearing what isn't said."
> Peter F. Drucker (American management guru)

11.2 Negotiation

Project Managers need to negotiate with many people during the project. For example, they will negotiate time overruns, cost overspends and quality tolerances with the Project Sponsor. They will negotiate with suppliers when agreeing contracts. They will negotiate with the team to agree objectives and timescales. They may need to negotiate with the team to persuade them to work overtime in order to meet a crucial project milestone; this will usually involve the negotiation of appropriate remuneration!

Negotiation has a set of standard steps:

Preparation: This is the most important step. Before holding a meeting with the other party, you need to consider the following:

- Your objectives and desired outcome
- How far you can compromise (and have you got the authority to do so)
- Which elements you cannot give way on
- What the other party's objectives are.

Discussion: This is the first activity in the negotiation meeting where each party will seek and give information about their position. It is important to listen carefully and watch body language as this will provide clues. You are trying to deduce what the other party's 'show-stoppers' are.

Proposal: This step involves each party suggesting that they move their position on elements of the negotiation. Each party is giving the other signals about which elements they are willing to alter. Statements such as, "If I do this, then will you do that?" will be made. It is important to not accept the first proposal made to you.

Bargaining: This is the most intense part of the process and both parties must pay full attention to what is said. Items are exchanged and concessions are made in the interest of striking a deal.

The last step of negotiation is to agree the final deal and probably to document the final outcome, depending on its complexity. If the final outcome does require documentation, then you have not closed the deal until the written agreement is confirmed by both parties (i.e., communication is two-way).

During the negotiation process, the Project Manager needs to show patience and resilience if the conversation gets a little difficult. Active listening will be required to fully understand the other party and try to reach a compromise.

11.3 Action-centred leadership

Dr. John Adair developed a model to explain the needs of a team working on a project. He identified the three main areas of need of the team as:

- Task: the need to get the job done
- Team: the need to build an effective team, and maintain it
- Individual: the need to treat people as individuals, and to develop their skills.

Adair said that achieving an equal balance between these three needs is crucial to creating a team with a high team morale and synergy.

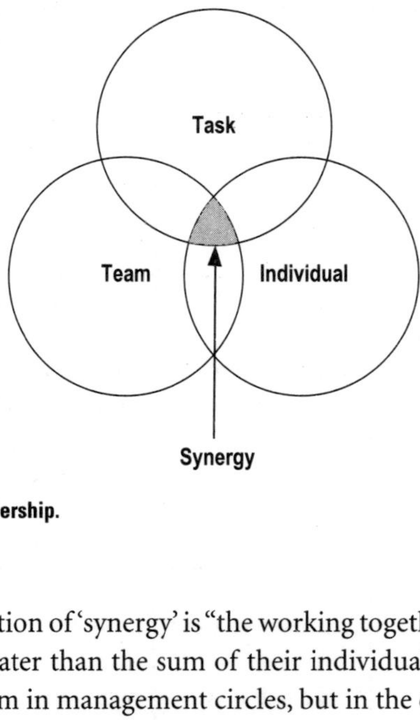

Figure 11.1: Action-centred leadership.

The dictionary definition of 'synergy' is "the working together of two or more things to produce an effect greater than the sum of their individual effects". It tends to be a somewhat over-used term in management circles, but in the context of team-building it is an important aim for the Project Manager. It means that a team is more effective than the sum of the individual team members. A team working with synergy will be showing signs such as helping each other with problem-solving, patiently explaining technicalities to each other, and taking joint responsibility.

To get the job done, the team needs clear objectives, a clear structure to its work, enough resources and effective communication. To have an effective team, the team members need clear objectives, full participation in the work, consensus in decision-making and regular communication.

Development of individuals requires understanding of what 'makes them tick', agreeing what the individual and the team leader can expect from each other, finding and using the strength of each individual, allowing for their weaknesses, listening to their opinions and problems, and giving positive feedback for good work.

11.4 Tuckman's model of team development

Tuckman's model shows the various stages that a team will go through, from the point where they are first brought together as individuals to (hopefully) the time when they are working with synergy.

One of Tuckman's key points is that when there are changes to the team, which could be someone new joining the team or someone leaving the team, the team reverts back to the forming stage. If this happens, it will probably take much less time than before for the team to progress through the stages, but the group dynamics have been

Stage	**Typical Behaviours**	**Typical Language**	**Project Manager's strategy**	**Required to move into next stage**
Forming	Polite. Watchful. Avoid sensitive issues. Keep personal issues private.	'Nice to meet you.' 'Can I get you a coffee?'	Structure the team. Give clear instructions.	Consensus about the team purpose. Understanding of the need to work as a team.
Storming	Arguing. Interrupting. Challenging the leader. Withdrawal by some people.	'You did that wrong.' 'Why are we doing it this way?'	Allow conflict. Intervene only when conflict may be serious. Brainstorm problems.	Conflicts to be resolved. A 'normal' way of working to have developed. Natural leaders identified.
Norming	Active listening. Participation by all. Self-disclosure. Socialising.	'This is the process we use here.' 'Let's see if we can resolve this.' 'Why don't we try this?'	Encourage. Look for consensus on decisions. Keep focus. Feedback.	Loyalty to the team. Commitment to the task. Understanding of personalities.
Performing	Synergy. Gets coffees without need for asking. Banter.	'Let me help you with that.' 'We're all responsible for this problem.'	Take a back seat. Allow joint decision-making. Use motivating factors.	

disrupted. A new member will need to find his way in the team, just as the existing members will need to get to know the person who has just joined the group.

> "Coming together is a beginning. Keeping together is progress. Working together is success."
> Henry Ford (founder of the Ford Motor Company)

The team cannot progress to the next stage unless the stage activities have been experienced properly. For example, if the Project Manager 'stamps' on all conflict situations during the Storming stage, the team members will feel that their conflicts remain unresolved. The team will not have enough joint confidence to be able to go forward into Norming.

11.5 Motivation

> "I praise loudly. I blame softly."
> Catherine the Great (1729–1796)

The Project Manager needs to motivate the team and the individual team members in order to get the best results from them. A motivated person will stay late to resolve a problem, will be keen to take on extra responsibility, and will even motivate others around him.

Motivation doesn't last. One day you can be feeling highly motivated and keen to get everything sorted out, and the next day you can be feeling that your motivation has diminished. So what happened? Maybe your manager said something very critical to you in public, or you got frustrated because you couldn't resolve a problem, or you have heard there are going to be redundancies in your organisation. Whatever it was, your motivation disappeared very quickly. So the Project Manager needs to keep motivational levels in all of the team 'topped up'.

Different people are motivated by different things. Some people are highly motivated by an extremely difficult challenge, whereas for others if a challenge is perceived as too difficult it could actually de-motivate them. Consider whether you have ever wanted to climb Everest. Would you even try? But maybe you could be out on a country walk, see a fairly challenging hill and be motivated to climb it because you believe that you can.

Frederick Herzberg had a theory about motivation, related to job satisfaction. He divided several factors into two groups: motivating factors (or 'satisfiers') and hygiene factors (or 'dissatisfiers'). He said that if the hygiene factors aren't there, you can't begin to move on to the motivating factors. So if you're worried about keeping up with the mortgage payments with the risk of losing your house, you will not be motivated by recognition at work. The basic need for food and shelter is far more pressing for a human being than any desire for career advancement.

Once you have all of the hygiene factors in place, they cannot motivate you. Other needs arise, such as the need for career advancement and more responsibility. So if

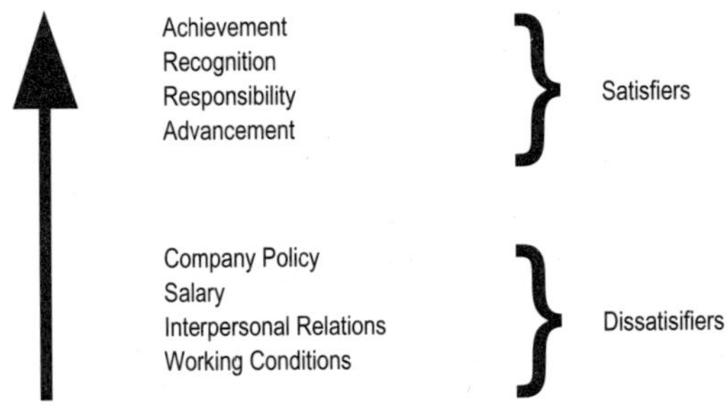

Figure 11.2: Herzberg's theory of motivation.

you are extremely satisfied with your working conditions, you look to other areas for advancement or progress.

The issue of salary is an interesting one; many people would say that their salary does motivate them but actually it usually depends on how they get paid. If you receive a monthly payment which is always the same (until the next pay review) then it is unlikely to motivate you to leap out of bed in the mornings with a huge smile and throw yourself into your work. However, money can be motivating if it represents a bonus to your expected pay. If you are promised a bonus on the basis that you deliver something by a certain date, this is more likely to motivate you. Being awarded an unexpected pay rise can fire up your motivation for a long time.

A Project Manager can use this theory by ensuring that the team members have the hygiene factors in place before trying to motivate them with the motivating factors. And once the hygiene factors are in place, as you would guess, a good strategy for motivating people is to concentrate on the motivating factors. So incentivise your staff with promises of more responsibility and career advancement, rather than a new cappuccino machine in the kitchen.

Like all 'people theory' models, this is only a model and will not be 100% accurate for all members of the team. But it provides a good basis for understanding the needs of your team when you discuss expectations (on both sides) with them, or when you are looking for them to put more effort into their work for the benefit of the project.

11.6 Leadership

There are different styles of leadership that a Project Manager can adopt during the project. The choice of style used will be affected by the personality of the Project Manager; it can be difficult to adopt a style that is alien to your natural way of leading. The situation will also have a great effect; consider the difference between an army major who needs to get his troops out of a dangerous position immediately, and a manager who needs a joint decision made about where to place the water cooler in the office.

The other factor which will affect the choice of style used is the development of the team being led. So returning to Tuckman's model, if the team is still in the Forming phase, then a highly directive but low supportive style of leadership will be needed.

People will need to be told what their job is and where they fit in. The team needs less structure as it moves into Storming, but still needs a high level of direction and support to deal with the increased levels of conflict. Once Norming is reached, the Project Manager can become less directive but still quite supportive. By the time the team is Performing, they are resolving their own disagreements and supporting each other very well, so they need much less support from the Project Manager. Figure 11.3

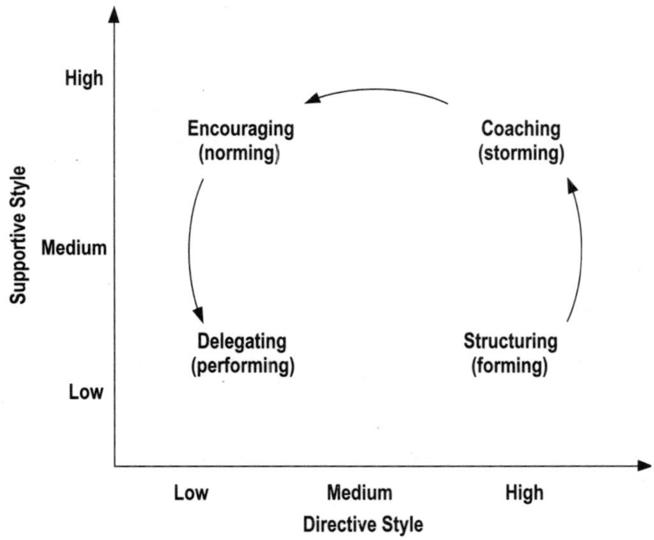

Figure 11.3: Leadership styles.

below shows this progression and gives names to the leadership styles at each of the four stages mentioned.

This can be used to adapt your style to fit the circumstances, and hence be a more effective and respected leader.

11.7 Conflict management

When a team of people with different personalities, strengths and weaknesses work together in a highly pressurised environment, conflict is inevitable. Some conflicts are minor and can be dealt with quickly and easily, others are major and need diplomacy, persistence and negotiation skills to be successfully resolved.

The Project Manager needs to be aware of the symptoms of conflict. These can be obvious, such as the raising of voices or full-blown arguments, or more subtle such as the feeling of tension in the air or people using 'them and us' implications in their speech.

Sources of conflict are wide-ranging:

- People have different agendas; for example, one person may wish the project to use a new technical tool so that he can add experience of that to their CV. This is likely to be a hidden agenda

- Personality clashes; people will always have different values, beliefs, interests and styles of working
- Age differences; these can cause widely different views and opinions
- Arguments about resources—technical experts or specific machinery.

In resolving conflict, the Project Manager has a choice of styles which are appropriate in different situations. Figure 11.4 below shows five different conflict management styles, based on two scales- how assertively and how co-operatively you are behaving:

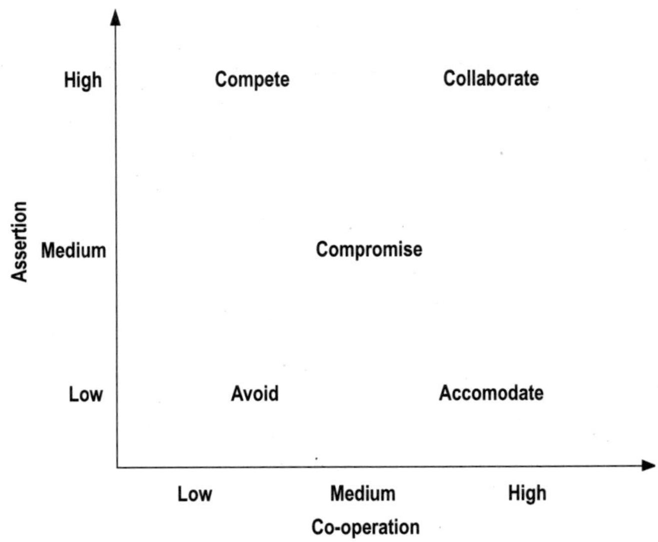

Figure 11.4: Conflict management styles.

Avoid: This is effectively ignoring the conflict. You may do this if the conflict is minor, or the team is currently in the Storming phase. If the conflict is between you and another party, then this approach is neither assertive nor co-operative and is therefore not very helpful.

Accommodate: This refers to a situation when there is conflict with another party and you decide to be very co-operative but not very assertive. You may do this when the Issue is not important to you, but very important to the other party, or when the other party is senior to you.

Compete: If you are feeling very assertive and not very co-operative, then you might put up a fight to win the argument. You might do this when you feel that you cannot possibly compromise, or when you have authority over the other party.

Collaborate: This is the highly co-operative, highly assertive option. If it is possible for both parties to collaborate, then this achieves a win:win, where neither party has had to give anything away to reach a resolution. This is not often possible in conflict situations.

Compromise: This is achieving a half-win:half-win because each party has had to give something away to reach a resolution of the conflict. This is more realistic and more common than collaboration. You may take this approach when the other party is in a similar position to yourself in terms of authority, or when you feel that negotiation will lead to a reasonable solution for both parties.

As we have already seen from Tuckman's model, levels of conflict vary within the project life cycle. Early on, the team will experience high levels of conflict when it is Storming. Hopefully as the project progresses, the team will reach Performing, when it will resolve most conflict internally, without it becoming visible to many others and without needing to involve the Project Manager.

11.8 Summary

In this chapter you have learnt:

- Communication requires feedback before it is complete
- Words are only 7% of the message
- Preparing for negotiation is crucial
- Effective leadership focuses equally on the task, team and individuals
- Team behaviours change as the team develops
- Leadership styles should adjust as the team develops
- Conflict varies with team development and can be managed in different ways.

This was the last chapter concerning the Implementation phase. The next chapter explains how to close down the project in an organised and controlled manner.

11.9 Practical assignment

Consider the following situations in the restaurant project. Decide what approach you would take to resolving these Issues.

1. The Head Chef, Willie Wok, has come to talk to you about one of the kitchen staff. The kitchen staff are currently undergoing staff training which involves many hours spent in the kitchen practising all of the menu ideas that have been generated. As the restaurant is not yet open for business, and the building work is incomplete, there is nowhere for the staff to sit and relax in their breaks. Most of them are fine about this but one of the cooks, Spike Spatula, is sighing a lot, always comes back from his breaks complaining loudly, and has been late for work on three occasions.

2. The restaurant manager, Nick Noodle, and one of the waitresses, Suzi Soy, are not speaking to each other. This has been going on for two weeks and has affected morale in the whole project as people are starting to take sides.

3. Once the kitchen staff and the waiting staff had been recruited and staff training had begun, you noticed how respectful everyone was with each other. But lately you've noticed that people have started to blame each other when things go wrong. The

more vocal members of the team have become more aggressive and the quiet ones have become withdrawn. Meanwhile there is an issue with the interface between the two teams. The waiting staff, led by the assertive Sally Spice, maintain that they should be able to walk around the kitchen to hurry the kitchen staff in their work if customers have been waiting a long time. The kitchen staff, led by the equally assertive Lemon Grass, maintain that this should not happen, as the kitchen is their domain.

11.10 Study

Answer the following multiple-choice questions. For answers see Appendix C.

1. If the Project Manager is too busy to worry about team-building, what is most likely to be the result?
   a) Team members being late for work after drunken nights out
   b) Good skills transfer between team members
   c) Technical problems
   d) Low morale.

2. Which one of the following statements is true?
   a) Conflict levels stay constant if the team members don't change
   b) Levels of conflict vary in the project life cycle
   c) Avoiding conflict is the most effective way to treat it
   d) The Project Manager should always stamp out conflict.

3. Which is the first step in negotiation?
   a) Preparation
   b) Bargaining
   c) Discussion
   d) Proposal.

4. Which would be the best way to communicate if a team is geographically remote?
   a) Videolink/web cam
   b) Telephone
   c) Email
   d) Reports.

The project manager's diary

People: unpredictable, irrational and with the power to really mess up a project. All sorts of problems have been going on. I used some of the people management models to sit and think through what I was going to do. I know that these models are only a general guide but I do find that they help when you feel really stuck on a people Issue.

So I used Herzberg's motivation theory to sort out Spike's behaviour. We managed to locate a room which is later going to be used as a store. It's not perfect but now the staff have a quiet rest area until the proper one is built.

The principles of negotiation helped me with preparing to manage the conflict between Nick and Suzi. It turned out to be a huge misunderstanding about what one of the team was supposed to have said about the other. In the end, once I had facilitated the meeting and impressed upon them the need for a peaceful resolution, they were very adult about it and I think we have a new working relationship being forged.

And good old Tuckman helped me to identify that the team were in the middle of Storming. I kept a watchful eye on them and eventually someone suggested a compromise, which one-by-one the other team members seemed to accept. The atmosphere is much more positive now and I believe the team have learnt that they can sort some things out for themselves without having to call me in all of the time as an adjudicator. Hopefully I can pull away a bit now and concentrate more on the publicity side of things which has a few problems.

I'll just make a note to hold some sort of night out for everyone once I think we're through Storming, to build on the success of reaching the Norming stage.

12 Handover and Closeout: Closing down the project properly

This chapter deals with the steps required to close down the project in a controlled manner. This is important because all stakeholders need to be kept informed that the project has closed, there needs to be a clear handover to Operations, and the project should not be allowed to drift.

A project is a temporary organisation, which means that at the end of the project the Project Manager will move on to another project, possibly in a different location with a different group of people and a different customer. The Project Manager will need to be focused on that new project. So what he doesn't want is a stream of constant interruptions from the people using the new products (the users) or from those operating and maintaining the new products (Operations). Sometimes the company accountants have numerous queries about the project finance information. It can be difficult, as well as frustrating, for the Project Manager to have to remember this information or where it can be found.

All of this means that the Project Manager needs to carry out a full and comprehensive closure of the project. This is the last phase of the project life cycle.

More specifically, Handover covers obtaining Customer Acceptance and transferring responsibility to Operations. The Post-Project Review is then carried out, followed by Closeout which covers planning the Benefits Realisation Review, dismantling the project infrastructure, releasing resources (human and machinery) and finalising the project costs.

12.1 Customer Acceptance

The project needs proof that the customer is happy with the new products. This means that the customer agrees that the Acceptance Criteria in the Quality Plan have been met by the project. Customer Acceptance can take many different forms: it could be an Acceptance Certificate signed by the customer; it could be the sum of all of the Acceptance Test Plans signed off by the customer as successful; it could be a formal letter from the customer.

Occasionally the project may obtain 'caveated acceptance'. This means that the customer signs up to having accepted the products 'with the caveat that …' where the caveat may be the completion of something fairly small such as a User Guide that just needs a small amount of work to complete it. Commercially, it can be preferable to close down the project with this small piece of work outstanding, rather than to keep the project open whilst one person completes this task.

12.2 Handover to operations

The group that is now going to operate and maintain the products will need to formally accept them. If the project has delivered an IT system, this would normally be the IT Support team. If the project has delivered a new building, this would be the Facilities Manager. If you have commissioned a builder to build you a new house, then this is the point where you go around the house with the builder and agree the 'snagging list', with a commitment from the builder to deal with them and sign them off later.

This implies that the operations team has been involved in the project throughout, and fully understands the project's products and their use. Certainly the Operations team should have been identified as a key stakeholder within the project and formal communications with it should have been planned in the Communication Plan.

If the project's products are going to be subject to updates in the future, for example, if the project has delivered an IT system, then the project's configuration database will be handed over to Operations as well.

The Project Board should not allow the project to close formally without this acceptance, as this would imply that the Operations team is not ready and as soon as issues with the new products occur, they may cause serious problems for the organisation. For example, if the users of a new IT system keep getting an error message and the Operations team don't know what it means or how to fix it, and if the system is critical to the business (such as an online booking system dealing directly with customers) then the implications could be very serious.

12.3 Post Project Review

Once we have obtained Customer Acceptance and handed over to Operations, the project closure activities can start.

The Post Project Review meeting, should review the achievements of the project against what was intended in the Project Management Plan. All of the contents of the Project Management Plan (PMP) should be reviewed so that the actual project can be compared with the planned project. In addition to the PMP, the Issue and Change Logs should be reviewed. These may provide useful information on what sort of unexpected Issues occurred, and also any Change Requests that the project did not implement due to lack of time or money, but which may be implemented later. If the Project Assurance roles prepared reports then these should be looked at again, along with progress reports from the Project Manager.

The output from the Post Project Review meeting should be an End Project Report, which will summarise the project results and the outputs from reviewing the project documentation. Typically the End Project Report will contain:

- Performance against timescale, including tolerance
- Performance against cost budget, including tolerance
- Performance against customer requirements
- Summary of approved changes and their effect on the Project Plan
- Summary of Issues raised
- Quality checking statistics.

12.4 Lessons Learned Report

During the project the Project Manager will have been noting down any lessons that were learned. For example, there may be technical lessons about a new tool that was used in the project, or lessons about the effectiveness (or otherwise) of one of the management processes, for example, the change control process. Maybe some new elements need to be added to the supplier selection process. Whether things went well or badly, there are always useful lessons to be gained from this information. At the very least, the Project Manager should list all of the task estimates against the actual effort required to complete each task. In this way, useful lessons can be learned about the accuracy of estimating, with the intention of improving this skill within the organisation.

So this information needs to be disseminated to the rest of the organisation. This happens via the Lessons Learned Report, which the Project Manager puts together and sends to the Quality Assurance (QA) function. The QA function updates the Quality Management System for the organisation according to the lessons learned, and then it is used by all Project Managers in the organisation as an input to the Quality Plan for their next project.

> "In the book of life, the answers aren't in the back."
> Charlie Brown (cartoon strip by Charles Schulz [1922–2000])

12.5 Benefits Realisation Review

When the project closes, and the new products are about to be used in a live environment for the first time, it is not usually possible to measure the business benefits in the Business Case. If the Business Case states that, for example, the project will make a profit of *x* in the first year of operation and a profit of *y* in the second year, then we have to go through those years in order to be certain that those figures have been achieved.

This causes a problem, because the project has closed but the ultimate success of the project—the business benefits—cannot be measured. This means that it is very easy to forget to carry out the Benefits Review. In many organisations measuring benefits is forgotten, or not given sufficient importance. Sometimes the Project Sponsor has left the organisation and has not handed this over to his successor.

So how can the Project Manager ensure that the Benefits Review will take place? One way is to make it clear to the Project Sponsor that it is his responsibility to do this. The Project Sponsor takes the business view of the project, and cannot be sure that the business has benefited from the project until the Benefits Review has happened. Another way is for the Project Manager to put together an agenda for the Benefits Review, covering date, attendees, benefits to be measured and method of measuring them. The Project Manager can give this agenda to the Project Sponsor with the project closure documentation. This will increase the chances of the Benefits Review taking place.

There are also some useful lessons that can be learned from the Benefits Review. By checking achievement of the benefits, what is really being tested is the assumption, made during the project Definition phase, that the specified functionality will achieve those benefits. If the benefits are not achieved, then further investigation of why the delivered functionality did not produce them will usually uncover some useful facts. For example, in the case study project the financial benefits may not be achieved because the current trend for Asian food is replaced by the emergence of (say) Middle Eastern cuisine. For the next restaurant, the owner may decide to spend more on market research to (hopefully) spot these trends.

12.6 Archive the files

The Project Manager must ensure that the project files are securely archived so that they can be audited in the future and available in case of any legal difficulty. Documentation should be retained in accordance with the retention policy of the organisation; in some cases, for example, the pharmaceutical industry, this may be as long as 25 years.

12.7 Reward the team

Whether or not the project has been a success in terms of meeting the constraints of time, cost and quality, the Project Manager should recognise the hard work put in by all the team members by arranging some sort of post-project event. It doesn't have to be fancy or expensive; a sum of money to spend at the local pub or curry house is often enough to let workers know that management appreciates their efforts, and to keep them motivated for the next challenge.

12.8 Summary

In this chapter you have learnt:

- The importance of a controlled closure of the project
- The elements of closing a project
- Some of the issues surrounding the Benefits Review.

12.9 Practical assignment

Based on the following information and the Project Plan, Quality Plan, Risk Log and Cost Account in Appendix B, produce an End Project Report for the restaurant project.

12.10 Study

Answer the following multiple-choice questions. For answers see Appendix C.

1. Which document is the key one to be reviewed in the Post Project Review?
   a) PMP
   b) Issue Log

c) Lessons Learned
d) Change Log.

2. The Lessons Learned Report should include:
   a) All useful information for the rest of the organisation
   b) What went badly on the project
   c) What went well on the project
   d) All of the above.

3 Who is the eventual recipient of the Lesson Learned Report?
   a) The Project Sponsor
   b) The Quality Assurance function
   c) It is archived
   d) Project Assurance.

4 Which of the following lives on after the project has closed?
   a) The Issue Log
   b) The Risk Log
   c) The configuration database
   d) The Project Plan.

The project manager's diary

Once the team had been through Storming and settled down to work together more effectively, we really started to motor though the tasks. I made a poster out of the milestones and stuck it on the wall, and it was so satisfying for all of us to see the milestones being ticked off as we met them.

The second stage boundary on 12 March was much better than the first. Charlie took it more seriously and imposed himself on the review. He actually asked some pertinent questions about how the risks were being managed and how the quality control process was working. By the time we got to the third stage boundary I felt that Charlie really understood that he owned the project. We did find that this was a useful time to review the publicity strategy and made a few changes in terms of which newspapers we were using.

The last stage was the hardest—we were all working every hour to ensure that the launch event would be successful. Once we'd sent out the invitations we'd committed to that date. Inevitably some of the tasks that had been planned to have been finished had been delayed, but not seriously. The interior build was on the critical path so this is where we focused most of our efforts. I was keen to keep the team motivated during this time so I made sure Charlie bought the pizzas in when we were all giving up our evenings and weekends.

May 14th:

My head hurts. Every word is taking too long to write. What a great time we had last night at the launch event. I need to write this slowly because my head is banging with a champagne-induced hangover, but I'm really elated by the way we all pulled together and created such a successful evening. The food was fantastic—the Chicken Pad Thai and the Penang Curry were mentioned by everyone and Charlie was in his element. And I got the bit of luck which every Project Manager deserves at some point—at the last minute I managed to get some Premiership footballers to attend! I even got Jim, who scored the winning goal for Liverpool in the cup, and the paparazzi were here—I think the pictures will be in the celebrity glossies next week. Plus a local golfer, something which really impressed Charlie.

All I need to do now is to finalise the End Project Report and Lessons Learned Report and archive the files. I've already produced the plan for the Benefits Review. I know that holding a Benefits Review is often forgotten but I've handed the plan to Charlie and it's up to him now to ensure that his business gains the advantages from carrying this out. He may find that the customer figures are not as good as we predicted, and this affects his revenue, but his organisation can learn some useful lessons from how we approached this issue on this project.

For the Lessons Learned Report I need to use all my diplomatic skills. Many of the project problems were caused by Charlie, for example, nearly changing to an American diner when we were well into the Implementation phase. And I think that Charlie's company could learn some useful lessons about agreeing a fixed price with a building contractor, as sometimes we got into contractual wranglings about interpretations of the design. And I will document how Glass Is Us tried to pull a fast one on the price of the window frames.

But overall it's been a great success and I'm sure that Nick Noodle will manage the restaurant competently. He's a sensible guy and accepted the project products with a great deal of pragmatism, as some of them were a little bit incomplete but nothing that affected the capability of the restaurant operation. It was key to the operational success of the restaurant that we recruited him early and got him working on the project.

So I'm nearly done here and then I'm off to catch a plane. Charlie has a mate in Indonesia who wants to launch a fish and chip restaurant.

Appendix A Case Study description

A.1 Background to the Case Study

The objective of the project is to launch a new restaurant. Charlie, the Project Sponsor, has recruited you to manage the project. He is the owner of the restaurant chain 'Charlie's with several other restaurants in neighbouring towns. The restaurant is to be housed on the site of an old 'greasy spoon' café, in the outskirts of a market town, on a major road with a few other shops around. The restaurant will serve Asian food such as Japanese, Chinese, Indonesian and Malaysian.

Your job is to produce a Project Management Plan and then deliver the project against that plan.

The scope of the project is to:

- **Make structural changes to the building.** You will need to contract this work to a building firm.
- **Develop menus.** This will be done by the Head Chef and his team, once you have recruited them.
- **Design the interior.** You will need to contract an interior design company to turn it into an up-market restaurant.
- **Market the restaurant.** You will need to advertise the new restaurant, focusing local attention on the launch event.
- **Recruit and train the staff.** You will need to contract a specialist catering recruitment agency to find potential staff, and you will need to interview the applicants.
- **Equip the restaurant.** You will need to manage this, advised by the Head Chef, once he has been recruited.
- **Hold a launch event.** You will organise this event, and need to make sure it is successful!

The project ends after the launch event and the Project Manager hands over to the Restaurant Manager who will also need to be recruited as part of the project.

A.2 Information for the Business Case

The following information is provided in support of your Business Case.

	Item	Cost
Development Costs:		
	Building work	£ 60,000
	Development of menus	£ 10,000
	Interior design	£ 15,000
	Recruitment	£ 15,000
	Training	£ 10,000

(continued)

(continued)

	Item	Cost
	Equipment/Furniture	£ 45,000
	Launch Event	£ 30,000
	Total Development Costs:	**£ 185,000**
Operational Costs (per month):		
	Salaries	£ 15,000
	Food and Wine	£ 10,000
	Marketing	£ 1,000
	Total Operational Costs (per month):	**£ 26,000**
Income (per month):		
	Average covers per night = 50	
	Average covers per month = 1,500	
	Average spend per cover = £ 25	
	Income per month	£ 37,000
	Total Income (per month):	**£ 37,000**

A.3 Information for project planning

Task Description	Duration (days)	No. Resources
Prepare building plans	10	1
Obtain planning permission	15	0
Engage builder	10	1
Exterior building work	25	4
Interior building work	15	4
Design interior	15	1
Research market	5	1
Generate ideas	5	2
Test menus	10	4
Select agency	2	1
Interview applicants	5	2
Train staff	20	5
Purchase equipment	15	2
Install equipment	3	4
Advertise launch event	20	1
Send launch invitations	5	1
Run test launch event	10	5
Hold launch night	5	5

(See also A.2 Information for the Business Case.)

Activity content

- **Make structural changes to the building.** This activity is made up of the following tasks:
  - Prepare building plans. This is estimated to last 10 days and will be undertaken by the Architect.
  - Obtain planning permission (and Building Regulations approval). This is estimated to last 15 days and will be undertaken by the local council (i.e., an external resource).
  - Engage builder. This is estimated to last 10 days and the Project Manager will do this.
  - Exterior building work. This is estimated to last 25 days and the Builder (and his 3 workers) will do this.
  - Interior building work. This is estimated to last 15 days and the Builder (and his 3 workers) will do this.

- **Develop menus.** This activity is made up of the following tasks:
  - Research market. This is estimated to last five days and the Head Chef will do this (once he has been recruited).
  - Generate ideas. This is estimated to last five days and the Head Chef will do this (once he has been recruited) working together with the Project Manager.
  - Test menus. This is estimated to last 10 days and the Head Chef (and his three Kitchen Staff) will do this (once they have all been recruited).

- **Design interior.** This activity is not made up of lower level tasks. This is estimated to last 15 days and the Interior Designer will do this (once he has been contracted).

- **Recruit and train the staff.** This activity is made up of the following tasks:
  - Select agency. This is estimated to last two days and the Project Manager will do this.
  - Interview applicants. This is estimated to last five days and the Recruitment Agent and the Project Manager will do this.
  - Train staff. This is estimated to last 20 days and the Head Chef (and his three Kitchen Staff) and the Project Manager will be involved in this.

- **Equip the restaurant**. This activity is made up of the following tasks:
  - Purchase equipment. This is estimated to last 15 days and the Head Chef (once he has been recruited) and the Project Manager will do this.
  - Install equipment. This is estimated to last three days and the Head Chef (and his three Kitchen Staff) will do this (once they have all been recruited). (This can be done in parallel with the Interior Building Work.)

- **Hold launch event.** This activity is made up of the following tasks:
  - Advertise launch event. This is estimated to last 20 days and the Project Manager will do this.
  - Send launch invitations. This is estimated to last five days and the Project Manager will do this.

- Run test launch event. This is estimated to last 10 days (as it includes all of the preparation) and the Project Manager, Head Chef (and his three Kitchen Staff) will do this.
- Hold launch night. This is estimated to last five days and the Project Manager, Head Chef (and his three Kitchen Staff) will do this.

Appendix B Case Study sample answers

Chapter 1—Project definition

Political:

- What legislative constraints are there on the design of the new restaurant?
- Are catering staff usually in an industrial union, and if so what will this mean to the working conditions and shifts?

Economic:

- Will local people still have enough money to eat out as much as they do presently, or are interest rates about to escalate?
- Is the restaurant going to be in an affluent area?
- What prices do people in the area currently pay when they eat out?

Sociological:

- Will people still want to eat out as much as they do presently?
- What are the most popular cuisines at the moment, and are they likely to remain popular?
- What is the most popular day/time for people to eat out?

Technical:

- Are there any developments in catering equipment that we should take note of?
- Can we engage with good quality builders to develop the site?
- Are there some good quality catering recruitment agencies to identify the staff?

Legal:

- What sort of contracts should we agree with our suppliers?
- Will we definitely be awarded planning permission?

Environmental:

- How will the Health and Safety Executive be involved?
- What are the latest trends in interior design?
- How will we ensure that the project and the restaurant is eco-friendly? Consider recycling, energy-efficient lighting and appliances.

Chapter 2—Business Case

Reasons:

- The owner of the site is looking for more investment opportunities.

Options:

- Do nothing; hold on to the site in case the value increases
- Sell the site
- Build a restaurant on the site
- Build another kind of shop on the site
- Selected option: build a restaurant on the site. This is in line with the owner's current business, and market research suggests that an Asian style restaurant would be successful in this area.

Benefits:

- Covers average 50 per night = 1,500 per month
- Average spend per cover = £25
- Income per month = £37,000 (=£444,000 per annum)
- Profit: Income—operating costs = £37,000–£24,000 = £13,000 per month.

Cost:

	Item	Cost
Development Costs:		
	Building work	£ 60,000
	Development of menus	£ 10,000
	Interior design	£ 15,000
	Recruitment	£ 15,000
	Training	£ 10,000
	Equipment/Furniture	£ 45,000
	Launch Event	£ 30,000
	Total Development Costs:	**£ 185,000**
Operational Costs (per month):		
	Salaries	£ 15,000
	Food and Wine	£ 10,000
	Marketing	£ 1,000
	Total Operational Costs (per month):	**£ 26,000**

Time:

- We have six months from now to launch the restaurant. The latest launch date is 30 June.

Risks:

- Market research figures may be wrong, impacting on the income projection
- Another restaurant may open close by, reducing the operating income
- We may not get planning permission, causing delays or cancellation
- We may have chosen an unpopular cuisine, reducing the operating income
- Building/interior décor/kitchen equipment costs may rise, reducing profit
- Salary costs may be underestimated, reducing the operating income.

Cost-benefit analysis:

Year	0	1	2	3	4	5
Costs	(185)	(288)	(288)	(288)	(288)	(288)
Benefits	0	444	444	444	444	444
Cash flow	(185)	156	156	156	156	156
Cumulative Cash flow	(185)	(29)	127	283	439	595

Breakeven is within year 2.

Conclusion: The project is viable, based on the current estimates.

Chapter 3—Planning

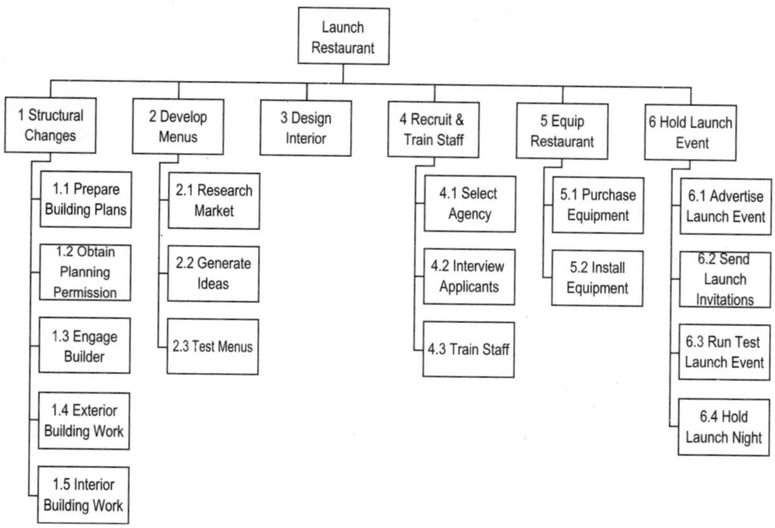

Figure B.1: Work Breakdown Structure.

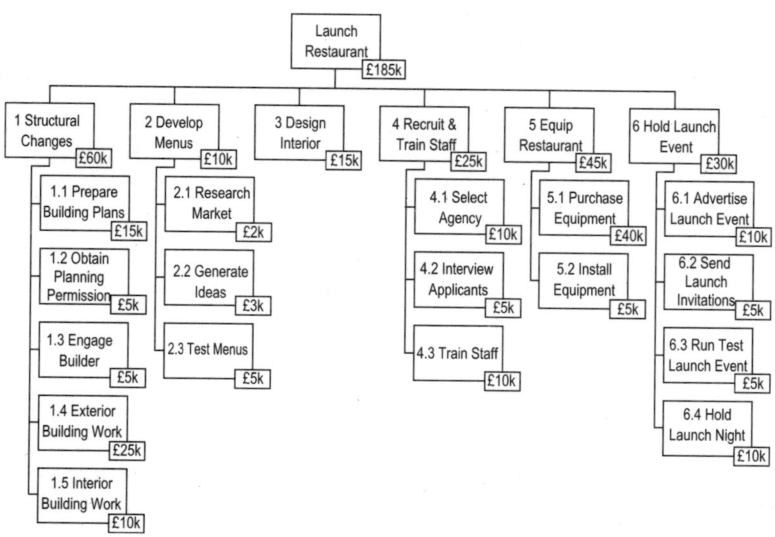

Figure B.2: Cost Breakdown Structure.

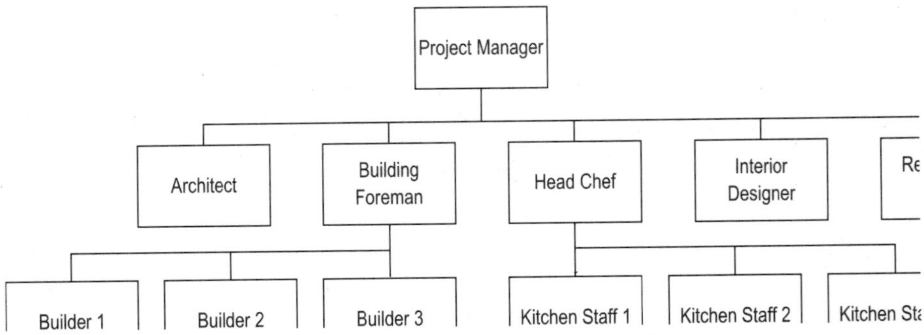

Figure B.3: Organisational Breakdown Structure.

Task Ref	Task Description	Project Manager	Architect	Building Foreman	Builders	Head Chef	Kitchen Staff	Interior Designer	Recruitment Agent
A	Prepare building plans	A	R						
B	Planning permission	A	R						
C	Engage builder	A, R	C						
D	Exterior building work	C, I		A	R				
E	Interior building work	C, I		A	R				
G	Research market	A				R			
H	Generate ideas	R, A				R			
I	Test menus	C, I				A, R	R		
F	Design interior	A		C				R	
K	Select agency	A, R							
L	Interview applicants	A, R							R
M	Train staff	A				R	R		
N	Purchase equipment	A		C		R			
O	Install equipment			A	R	C, I			
P	Advertise launch event	A, R				C			
Q	Send launch invitations	A, R							
R	Run test launch event	A, R				C	I		
S	Hold launch night	A, R				C	I		

Figure B.4: Responsibility Assignment Matrix.

Note: You may envisage other dependencies between some of the tasks. This diagram is correct, based on the information supplied in Appendix A. Once the diagram has been drawn, it provides a useful basis for checking understanding, and changes can be made if necessary.

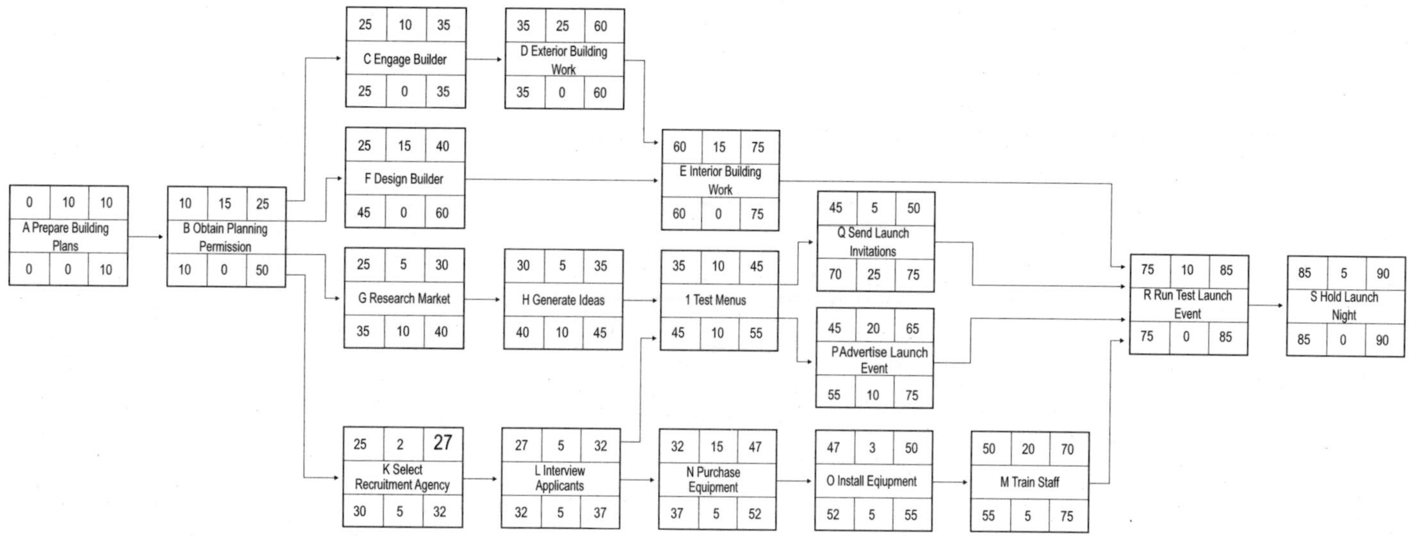

Figure B.5: Network diagram with critical path analysis.

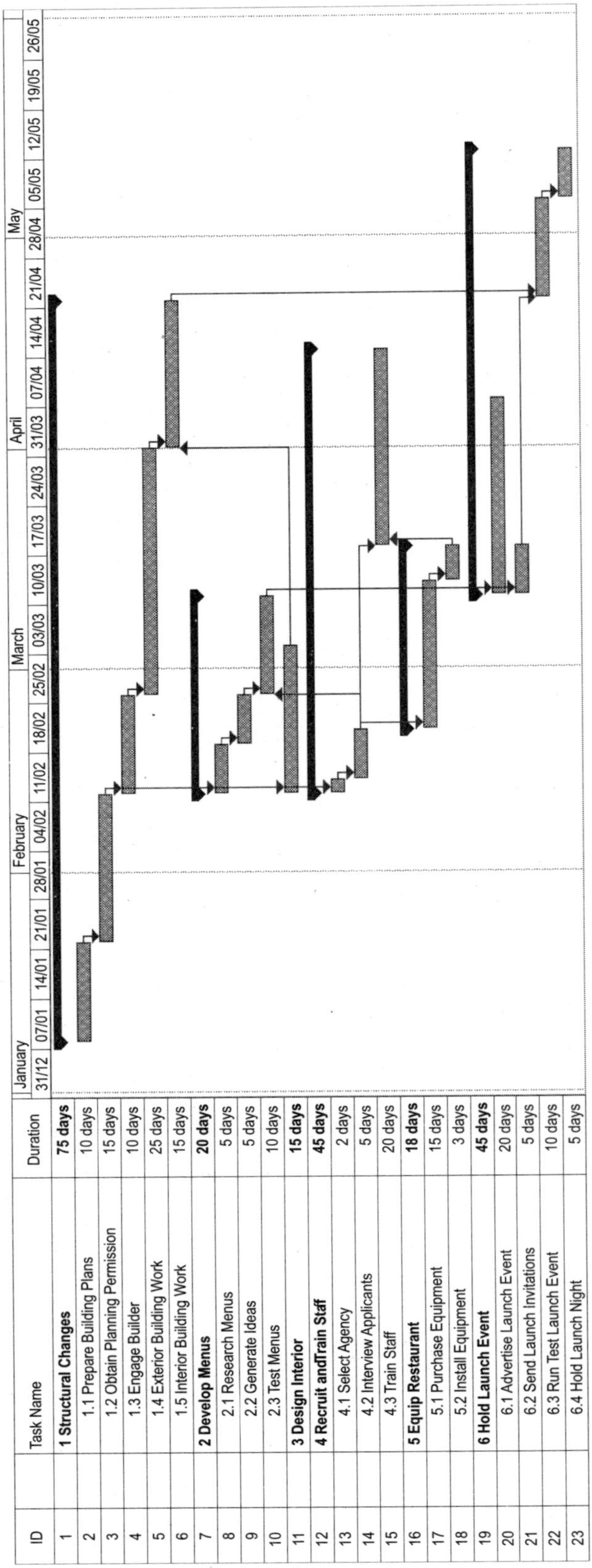

Figure B.6: Gantt chart.

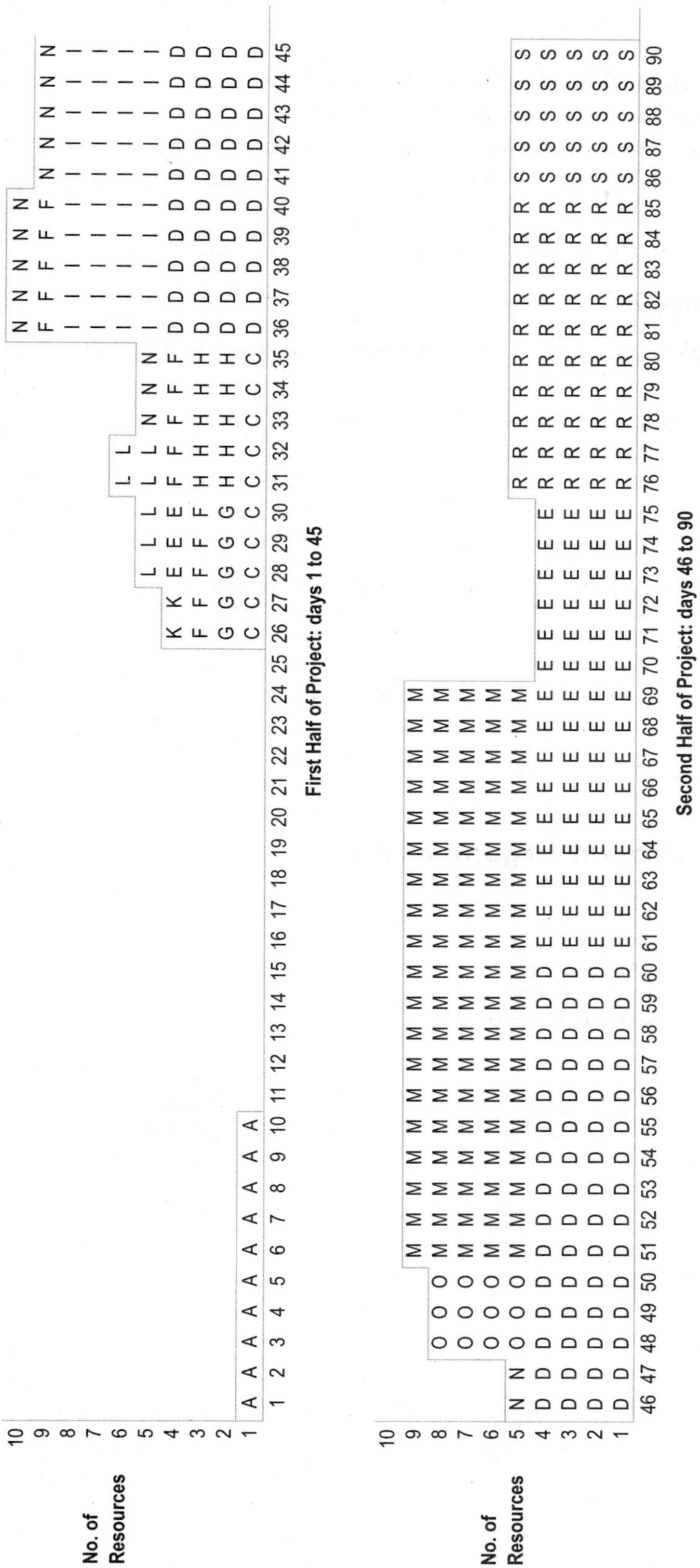

Figure B.7: Resource histogram.

Assumptions

- Planning permission takes only 15 days to be granted
- Planning permission will be granted on the first attempt
- We can find and contract with a builder, easily and quickly
- The agency we select will be able to find a good standard of experienced applicants
- Sufficient numbers of local people will want to attend the launch event.

External dependencies

- Health and Safety Executive (HSE)—dependent on them for inspections and certification
- Local celebrities who will be invited to the launch event
- Local council for planning permission.

Exclusions

- The only marketing that will be carried out is marketing the launch event.

Chapter 4—Project organisation

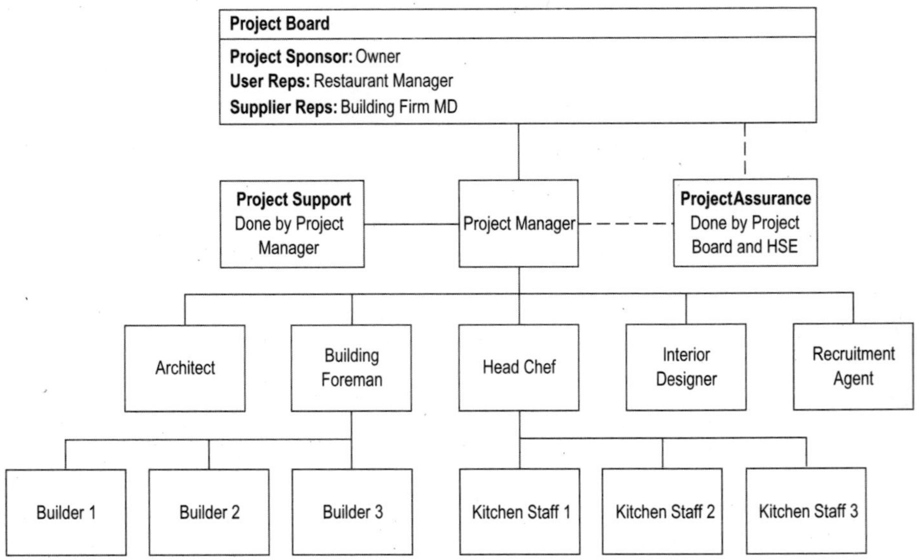

Chapter 5—Stakeholder management

Stakeholder analysis

Stakeholder	Success Criteria	Success Factors
Project Sponsor	Business benefits achieved	Focus on Business Case throughout
Building firm *	Profit	Estimate thoroughly and charge all change requests to customer
Interior design co. *	Profit	Estimate thoroughly and charge all change requests to customer
Restaurant manager	Well set-up restaurant	Ensure industry standard training and equipment are procured
Head Chef	Well-trained staff, good equipment, interesting menus	Ensure industry-standard training and equipment are procured, ensure menu development is innovative and creative
Recruitment agency *	Profit	Estimate thoroughly and charge all change requests to customer
Kitchen staff	Good training, good kitchen equipment	Ensure industry-standard training and equipment are procured
Local residents	Positive impact on local area. Minimal disruption	Ensure builders minimise disruption
Customers	Good food, good value, interesting menu	Ensure market research covers these areas
Local press *	Advertising revenue	
Architect *	Profit. Pictures in the architectural press	Recommendations and further commissions. Ensure enough margin in estimate
Local council	Building matches approved design	Ensure building firm is responsible for building exactly to the specification
HSE	No Health & Safety (H&S) problems	Ensure building firm takes responsibility for H&S

Note: For suppliers, marked *, the success factors are written from their perspective, as we are trying to understand what they might do to ensure achievement of their own success criteria.

Communication Plan

Stakeholder	Information Needs	Communication Method	Timing	Responsible	Feedback Route
Project Sponsor	Updates on time, cost quality and Business Case	Meeting and report	Weekly	Project Manager	Via meeting or raising Issues
Building firm	Current specification	Project Manager's meeting and documentation and Architect's documentation	Weekly with Building Foreman	Project Manager	Via meeting or raising Issues
Interior design company	Current specification	Project Manager's meeting and documentation	Weekly	Project Manager	Via meeting or raising Issues
Restaurant manager	Menus, launch date	Project Manager's meeting	Weekly	Project Manager	Via meeting or raising Issues
Head Chef	Project progress, esp. recruitment and delivery of equipment	Project Manager's meeting	Weekly	Project Manager	Via meeting or raising Issues
Recruitment agency	Current specification	Project Manager's meeting	Weekly	Project Manager	Via meeting or raising Issues
Kitchen staff	Job specifications, menu information, launch date	Progress meetings	Weekly	Head Chef	Via meeting or raising Issues
Local residents	General restaurant information	Press coverage	12 weeks before launch	Project Sponsor	Via P.O. box for Project Sponsor
Customers	Cuisine, pricing and launch date	Press advertising leaflets	Four weeks before launch	Project Manager	none
Local press	Advert information and launch invitations	Telephone and letter	One-off, eight weeks before launch	Project Manager	none
Architect	Interior design	Project Manager's meeting	Weekly, until design approved	Project Manager	Via meeting or raising Issues
Local council	Final design	Planning application	One-off	Architect	Via application process
HSE	HSE standards are being adhered to	Audits	Ad-hoc or if complaints are received	Project Manager and Building Foreman	Official HSE report

Chapter 6—Risk management

Risk log

Risk No.	Description	Prob.	Impact	Risk Score	Possible Actions	Cost of Action(s)	Selected Action(s)	Owner
1	Builders are late completing construction	3	3	9	Reduce—manage builders carefully, check progress reports against stage targets, ensure foreman produces good plan Transfer—have a penalty clause or bonus clause (or both) in the contract with the builders	0, £100	Reduce and Transfer	Building Foreman
2	Cannot find a decent Chef	2	2	4	Reduce—employ an agency to do this Contingency—if it happens, re-recruit (but this may be too late for the business)	£2,000	Reduce	Project Manager
3	Business Case: predictions of customer numbers too optimistic	2	3	6	Employ market research company to ensure type of restaurant will be well-received	£3,000	Reduce	Marketing Dept.

(continued)

(continued)

Risk No.	Description	Prob.	Impact	Risk Score	Possible Actions	Cost of Action(s)	Selected Action(s)	Owner
4	Project Manager is too overworked to concentrate on this project	1	2	2	Reduce—have a full-time deputy Project Manager to share workload Accept—as risk is low and reduction plan is very expensive	0	Accept	Project Manager
5	Health and Safety Executive close us down	1	3	3	Reduce—ensure Health and Safety constraints are built into Architect's plans for the building. Obtain advice from a catering industry H&S expert Accept—as risk is low, but cannot 'do nothing' as this is such high impact	£2,000	Reduce	Project Manager
6	Staff training, which is a critical path activity, is delayed or overruns	2	3	6	Reduce—split the staff training so that it is no longer on the critical path	0	Reduce	Training Consultant
7	Recruitment costs escalate	2	2	4	Fixed price contract to agency	0	Transfer	Procurement Manager

Risk No.	Description	Prob.	Impact	Risk Score	Possible Actions	Cost of Action(s)	Selected Action(s)	Owner
8	Local residents are unhappy about car-parking by customers	2	1	2	Contingency—offer discounts to local residents	£500	Contingency	Restaurant Manager
9	OPP—Restaurant attracts more customers than predicted in Business Case	2	2	4	Develop—research the market for types of food currently fashionable and ensure Chef is expert in those areas Ignore—could do nothing, but a small effort here may bring great benefits Share—put the Chef on a bonus scheme Share—put the Interior Designer on a bonus based on future customer feedback	£1,000	Develop (This plan increases the probability of occurrence most.)	Recruitment agency
10	OPP—We can accommodate more diners than estimated in the Business Case	2	2	4	Develop—investigate different arrangements of tables	£1,000	Develop	Interior Designer

- Total Cost of Risk Actions £9,100
- Total Contingency Budget £500
- NB 'status' column is not shown as all risks are 'current' in the initial Risk Log.

Chapter 7—Quality management

Project quality plan

Customer's requirements

The restaurant is to hold a maximum of 40 diners. The building and interior are to be attractive with an interesting Asian-style menu, similar to the existing restaurant in Noodletown.

The restaurant kitchen and staff must be well organised and able to deal efficiently with 40 diners simultaneously.

Local celebrities are to be invited to the launch event.

The launch event must be held no later than 30 June this year. The development costs must not exceed £210,000. (Note: these are cost and time constraints, but they are also requirements of the customer and will have an impact on quality.)

Positive reviews of the restaurant must appear in the local press. There must be no serious complaints; only one minor complaint per month allowed.

Industry standards applicable to this project

Health and safety.

Building standards.

Catering standards.

Company (customer) standards applicable to this project

The company Quality Management Systems (QMS) applies to this project.

How to apply the required standards to this project

Health and Safety standards will be applied by the Building Foreman to all construction activities. Building Standards will be applied by the Building Control Inspector to the works in progress. Catering Standards will be applied by the Head Chef in all catering activities.

Quality checking strategy

Management products: to be approved by the Project Sponsor.

Building products: to be approved against samples provided before delivery by the Building Foreman and his team.

Catering products: to be approved by the Head Chef and his team.

Design products: to be approved by the Project Sponsor, after a formal review involving the whole Project Management team.

Involvement of QA

The company's Quality Assurance team will perform ad-hoc audits of all of the management and technical activities, and will report their findings directly to the Project Sponsor.

Quality responsibilities in the project

Project manager:

- Ensuring everyone understands the quality check process
- Ensuring Product Specifications are signed off before work starts on development of the product
- Ensuring all products are approved before being used and records kept of all tests.

Project board:

- Overall achievement of quality
- Assurance of quality via Project Assurance.

User representative:

- Approval of all Product Specifications before products developed
- Approval of completed products.

Building foreman:

- Ensuring that building firm's own supplier standards are maintained.

Chapter 8—Configuration management

Configuration management plan

How the configuration will be managed

The configuration database will be managed using a simple MS-Excel spreadsheet. For each version of each product, the following information will be maintained:

- Product Id
- Version No
- Status
- Location
- Owner
- Issue Log ref
- Related products.

How versions of products will be uniquely identified

The unique reference of each row in the configuration database will be 'Product Id./ Version No.'.

The project filing structure

- Signed-off documents will be kept in the filing cabinet marked 'Restaurant' in the Project Office
- Electronic documents will be filed in one of three folders on the company server:
    - Folder 'Documents/Restaurant1/Management/Project' for management products such as the Business Case and Risk Log
    - Folder 'Documents/Restaurant1/Management/Quality' for quality products such as the Quality Plan and Quality Log

- Folder 'Documents/Restaurant1/Technical' for specialist products such as the Architect's Design and Launch Invitations.

What security will there be on filing items in the filing structure?

Only the Project Manager can file products. Only the Project Manager will be allowed access to the folders.

What security will there be on retrieving items from the files?

Only the Project Manager can retrieve products and distribute them. Only the Project Manager will be allowed access to the folders.

Who will be responsible for configuration management?

The Project Manager is responsible for the successful implementation of configuration management. Project Assurance (i.e., the Project Board) will carry out regular configuration audits to verify the database.

Who will operate the configuration management system?

As this is a relatively small project in terms of the number of configuration items, the Project Manager will carry out the functions of Control and Status Accounting.

Chapter 9—Change management

Change request impact analysis

Description of change

Change the restaurant to an American diner.

What needs to be changed?

- Menu research has already been done. This will need to be re-done, as we have researched the Asian style menus
- We were about to start generation of menu ideas, and next week we planned to be testing the ideas, so this change request needs to be decided upon quickly to avoid more impact
- Interior design has already started. This will need to be re-started, as it has been based on Asia
- We are just about to order the equipment. Some of this will have to change, as American food needs different equipment from Asian food
- Management products that will change: Project Plan, Business Case, Risk Log, current Stage Plan, Quality Log.

Justification for the change

- Increase in income of 10% is predicted. This is not time-limited.

Time impact

- Interior design and the research, ideas and testing of menus are not on the Critical Path so the project will not be delayed by these tasks. However, if this is not agreed within the next two weeks then the menu development work may become critical (there are 10 days' Total Float available on this work).

Cost of change

- Menu research: we have spent 25% of the budget of £10,000. Cost: £2,500
- Interior design: we have spent a third of the £15,000 budget. Cost: £5,000
- As the work should not delay the project, the cost of Project Management should not rise.

Impact on performance or quality

- No direct impact, but we may be tempted to cut corners in order to meet cost and time constraints, and hence reduce the quality of the final product.

Impact on business benefits

- An increase of 10% income will increase the profit by £3.7K per month, or £44.4K per annum
- Break even point for the project will now be within year 1, instead of year 2.

Impact on risks

- Making such a drastic change at this point makes the project risky. Non-critical tasks may become critical if they are delayed. There will be an increased risk of missing the launch date
- There is a risk that the Interior Designer we have employed may not be available if the work is extended.

Do we have the resources to make the change?

- Menu development is performed by project staff, so we do have the resources
- Interior design is being carried out by the external Interior Designer, so we will have to check his availability and extend his contract.

Chapter 10—Controls

Project stages

Stage	Start	End	Reasoning
1	08 Jan	09 Feb	Sensible to have a stage boundary just before the project contracts with the builder and the Interior Designer. The Project Board can ensure that everything is on track and the project remains viable before commitment is made.
2	12 Feb	09 Mar	On 12 March we are planning to send out the invitations to the launch. This is a 'point of no return' for the project as it involves publicity. Before the project commits to the launch date, we need to have a

(continued)

(continued)

Stage	Start	End	Reasoning
			management review of all progress, risks, Issues and quality to be as sure as possible that we can meet the date. We could move the launch date at this stage boundary if we need to.
3	12 Mar	30 Mar	This is a short stage but if we don't break up the rest of the project it would be a very long stage, and therefore the Project Board would not have enough control over the project. It would be sensible to have a management review here to ensure that the publicity is working, so that we can change the publicity strategy if we need to.
4	2 Apr	14 May	This is the last stage. Following successful launch, the Project Board will authorise the Project Manager to proceed into Handover and Closeout.

Cost account (all costs in £k)

		Estimates		
Item ref.	**Item**	**Labour Cost**	**Material Cost**	**Total Cost**
1.1	Building plans	15		15
1.2	Obtain planning perm.	5		5
1.3	Engage builder	5		5
1.4	Exterior building work	15	10	25
1.5	Interior building work	5	5	10
1	**Structural Changes**			**60**
2.1	Market research	2		2
2.2	Generate ideas	3		3
2.3	Test menus	3	2	5
2	**Develop Menus**			**10**
3	**Design Interior**	**15**		**15**
4.1	Select agency	10		10
4.2	Interview applicants	5		5
4.3	Train staff	8	2	10
4	**Recruit and Train Staff**			**25**
5.1	Purchase equipment		40	40
5.2	Install equipment	5		5
5	**Equip Restaurant**			**45**
6.1	Advertise launch event	8	2	10

(continued)

(continued)

		Estimates		
Item ref.	**Item**	**Labour Cost**	**Material Cost**	**Total Cost**
6.2	Send launch invitations	2	3	5
6.3	Run test launch event	4	1	5
6.4	Hold launch night	8	2	10
6	**Hold Launch Event**			**30**
	Risk Actions			9.1
	Project Management			4.5
	Total Planned Work			**198.6**
	Contingency budget			0.5
	Change budget			8
	Total Cost Budget			**207.1**

Chapter 11 – People management

1. Spike Spatula is de-motivated because of the working conditions. There is no point in trying to motivate him with responsibility, recognition or career advancement. This is a hygiene factor and needs to be rectified as soon as possible. The Project Manager should find somewhere for a staff rest area. If this means an increase in project cost then the Project Sponsor should be consulted.

2. This is a personality clash between two of the team. As it has become destructive and the staff involved show no signs of sorting it out themselves, the Project Manager needs to intervene. The Project Manager should take them into a room and:

   - Let Nick and Suzi know why intervention has been necessary
   - Use active listening to listen to both sides
   - Give both parties time to speak
   - Make it clear that a resolution is required; be firm but fair
   - Ask probing questions
   - Get them to suggest a solution
   - Facilitate a compromise
   - Get them both to agree the outcome and ensure it is unambiguous.

3. The team are in the 'Storming' phase. The Project Manager should allow the conflict to occur in the hope that the team can resolve it, and thus build up some trust in themselves as a team. If the Project Manager intervenes too early, the team may get stuck in the storming phase with unresolved Issues. The Project Manager needs to monitor the conflict and only intervene if it

becomes destructive. The leadership style used by the Project Manager should be Coaching.

Chapter 12—Handover and closeout

End Project Report

Performance against timescale, including tolerance

- Project plan was 90 days, but agreed timescale was 6 months (120 days). Therefore the time tolerance was 30 days. The original planned launch night was Saturday 13th May.
- This date was met. No time tolerance was spent.

Performance against cost budget, including tolerance

- Total cost of planned activities was £198.6K
- Change budget was £8K
- Contingency budget was £0.5K
- Total available budget was £207.1K
- Total planned activities cost more than planned due to the increased cost of building materials: increase of £5K.
- £5K of the Change Budget of £8K was spent on the change to the interior design, leaving £3K unspent.
- The Contingency Budget was spent—risk number eight occurred, resulting in a cost of £500.
- So overall the project overspent by £2K. But this was within cost tolerance. Customer specified maximum cost of £210K.

Performance against customer requirements

- All of the customer requirements were met.
- The customer did need persuading that the local second division football team were 'celebrities'. The reviews of the restaurant in the local press were mainly positive, and any Issues raised there have been addressed via staff training.

Summary of approved changes and their effect on the project plan

- The only implemented change was the change number 14, to the interior design. This cost £5K but was funded from the Change Budget. It caused a delay to the interior design task, but this was only 5 days. It did not affect the project timescale as it was not on the critical path.
- The proposed change to the restaurant style was not approved as it was deemed to be too risky at the late stage that it was suggested.

Summary of issues raised

- Most of the Issues were minor and handled by the Project Manager. The only one which caused tolerance to be exceeded, and was therefore raised to the attention of the Project Board, was the cost of building materials. This meant an increase to the cost of that stage of £5K.

Quality checking statistics

- Quality checking was performed in accordance with the Quality Plan. The Quality Log was used correctly as an audit trail of all quality checking work performed.
- The table below summarises the quality checking work:

Product group	No. of products	Role Responsible	No. of reviews passed first time	No. of products requiring major re-work
Building	32	Building Foreman	30	0
Catering	15	Head Chef	8	0
Design	4	Architect/Interior Designer	3	1

Appendix C
Multiple-Choice Answers

Chapter 1—Project Definition

1. c
2. a
3. d
4. b
5. b
6. a.

Chapter 2—Business Case

1. b
2. d
3. a
4. c.

Chapter 3—Planning

1. b
2. d
3. b
4. d
5. a
6. c.

Chapter 4—Project Organisation

1. c
2. a
3. d
4. b.

Chapter 5—Stakeholder Management

1. d
2. a
3. b
4. a.

Chapter 6—Risk Management

1. d
2. a
3. c
4. d
5. a
6. c.

Chapter 7—Quality Management

1. a
2. b
3. a
4. b.

Chapter 8—Configuration Management

1. c
2. d
3. a
4. a.

Chapter 9—Change Management

1. d
2. d
3. a
4. c.

Chapter 10—Controls

1. d
2. a
3. d
4. c.

Chapter 11—People Management

1. d
2. b
3. a
4. a.

Chapter 12—Handover and Closeout

1. a
2. d
3. b
4. c.

Appendix D Websites and further reading

D.1 Websites

www.projectivity.co.uk

The author's company website. Projectivity Ltd offers bespoke Project Management training, accredited PRINCE2 and Association for Project Management (APM) training in conjunction with preferred partners, consultancy in programme management, and project management, web design and web hosting services.

This website complements this book by providing further multiple-choice questions to test your Project Management knowledge in line with the APM Introductory Certificate, downloadable templates for the key Project Management documents.

www.apm.org.uk

United Kingdom based organisation dedicated to advancing the science of Project Management and the professional development of Project Managers. The Association of Project Management (APM) is the largest independent professional body of its kind in Europe, with over 15,000 individual and 400 corporate members throughout the UK and abroad. Their aim is to develop and promote Project Management across all sectors of industry and beyond.

www.ipma.ch

Homepage of the International Project Management Association (IPMA). This is a non-profit organisation, based in Switzerland, which aims to be a prime promoter of Project Management internationally through a membership network of national Project Management associations around the world. You can find out more about its history, events and membership on the website.

www.apmgroup.co.uk

The APM Group Ltd (APMG) specialises in the accreditation and certification of organisations, processes and people, within a range of industries and management disciplines.

www.prince2.org.uk

PRINCE2 is a process-based approach for Project Management providing an easily tailored and scaleable method for the management of all types of projects. The method is the de-facto standard for Project Management in the UK and is practised worldwide.

This website is all about the PRINCE2 methodology—what it is, who owns the method, which qualifications are available and who you can contact for training and consultancy.

www.programmes.org

Managing Successful Programmes comprises a set of principles and processes for use when managing a programme. It is founded on best practice although it is not prescriptive. It is very flexible and designed to be adapted to meet the needs of local circumstances.

This website is all about the Managing Successful Programmes (MSP) methodology—what it is, who owns the method, which qualifications are available and who you can contact for training and consultancy.

D.2 Further reading

APM Body of Knowledge

The *APM Body of Knowledge* is a sourcebook of Project Management knowledge and good practice and is written in a clear and accessible style and structured for easy access and use. The new fifth edition includes definitions and further reading for each updated Project Management knowledge area (or topic), a glossary of Project Management terms and an index.

ISBN: 1903494133

Managing Successful Projects with PRINCE2

This reference manual describes the PRINCE2 Project Management method which provides detailed guidance on how to set up, organise, manage, control and deliver your projects on time, within budget and to the right quality.

Author: Office of Government Commerce (OGC)
Publisher: TSO (The Stationery Office)
ISBN: 0113309465

Contracting for Project Management

This new book concentrates specifically on the contracting issues that surround projects of any size. A knowledge of contracting specifically for Project Management is essential if a project is to avoid difficulties and reach a successful conclusion.

Edited by J. Rodney Turner
ISBN: 0566085291

Practical Techniques for Effective Project Investment Appraisal (A hawksmere report)

The text contains many examples of appraisal process spreadsheets, designed to be of practical use in your business. In addition, detailed checklists mean you won't overlook any factors during the appraisal process.

by Ralph Tiffin
ISBN-10: 1854180991

Leadership: Theory and Practice

For anyone seeking to explore how an understanding of leadership theory can inform and direct the way leadership is practiced, the fourth edition of *Leadership: Theory and Practice* is an indispensable tool. Adopted as a textbook at over 250 colleges and universities, this bestselling volume is equally useful for private-sector leadership development training programs.

Author: Peter Guy Northouse

ISBN-10: 141294161X

The Definitive Book of Body Language: How to Read Others' Attitudes by their Gestures

Find out: how to tell if someone is lying, how to make yourself likeable, how to get co-operation from other people, how to interview and negotiate successfully, and how to choose a partner.

Authors: Allan Pease and Barbara Pease

ISBN-10: 0752858785

Glossary

Audit: A review of the project usually carried out by an independent body, such as Quality Assurance or external consultants.

Backward Pass: The process of calculating the bottom row of each Node whilst carrying out Critical Path Analysis.

Baseline: The approved starting position against which progress can be measured, e.g., a baseline Project Plan.

Benefits: The ultimate drivers of a project; the advantages brought into the organisation by the project.

Benefits Realisation Review: The formal measurement of achievement of the project benefits, held after the project's products have been used.

Bottom-up Estimating: The process of estimating each lowest-level task and then summing them to produce a total project estimate.

Budget: The amount of time or money set against a project or task, which represents the maximum allowed spend.

Business as Usual (BAU): The normal operations of an organisation, to which projects may implement a change.

Business Case: The management product which justifies the project on the basis of the expected benefits cost, time and risks versus

Change Authority: The group or person authorised to approve Change Requests.

Change Log: A log of all Change Requests raised on the project, to be kept up-to-date throughout.

Change Request: A formal request to change any previously agreed aspect of a project.

Closeout: The last phase of the project; carried out when all activities have been completed (or the project has terminated prematurely).

Comparative Estimating: An approach to estimating where the work to be done is compared with some previously completed similar work.

Conception: The first phase of the project, which establishes the options available and the viability of each option.

Configuration: The sum total of all products in the project, including management documents.

Configuration Database: The table of Configuration Items that is maintained by the Configuration Librarian. A new Configuration Item is added for every new version of a product.

Configuration Item: The information required about a version of a product, such as its status, location, owner and related products.

Contingency: An action planned to be carried out when a risk occurs.

Contingency Budget: An allowance set aside against the risks which have contingency actions planned for them.

Cost Account: A table of the cost breakdown of the project, showing planned labour and materials costs, allowances, Project Management and any other management allowances.

Cost Breakdown Structure (CBS): Hierarchical breakdown of the cost of the project; usually based on the Work Breakdown Structure (WBS).

Communication Plan: The strategy for ensuring that all stakeholders are kept informed. Each type of formal communication event should be listed.

Cost Benefit Analysis: The process of analysing the relationship between costs and benefits over a period of years, as a result of a project. Part of the Business Case.

Critical Path Analysis: The process of finding the longest path through the precedence network. It is often the path with zero total float on all tasks.

Customer Acceptance: The formal acceptance of the end result of the project by the body which has specified the requirements and paid for the project.

Definition: The second phase of the project. The project is defined, organised and planned and the Project Management Plan (PMP) is produced.

Definition Phase Plan: A plan produced during Conception which shows the cost and time for the Definition phase.

Dependency Network: A network of tasks showing the dependencies between them. The most common type of dependency is 'finish-to-start'.

Duration: The amount of time elapsed on a task.

Earliest Finish Time: The earliest possible time that an activity can finish, given its Duration and Earliest Start Time.

Earliest Start Time: The earliest possible time that an activity can start, given the constraints imposed by preceding tasks in the network.

Effort: The amount of hours or days required to carry out a task.

End Project Report: The output from the formal meeting to review the project's success.

Estimate: A quantitative prediction of the cost, effort or duration of a task.

Finish-to-Start Dependency: A precedence relationship between two tasks, where the second task cannot start until the first task is complete.

Forming: The first stage in Tuckman's model of team development.

Forward Pass: The process of calculating the top row of each Node whilst carrying out Critical Path Analysis.

Free Float: The amount by which an activity can be delayed without affecting any dependent activities.

Gantt Chart: A bar chart showing activities scheduled against a timescale. It can also show task dependencies, assigned resources and the critical path.

Gate Review: The management review of the project held at the end of one stage and the start of another. A business decision to continue or close the project is made, based on progress so far, future plans and any changes to circumstances.

Handover: The process of transferring ownership and management of the project's products to the Operations team.

Implementation: The third and largest phase of the project. The work is carried out according to the Project Management Plan (PMP). It is usually broken down into Stages.

Issue: A problem that requires resolution before it affects the project's chances of success. (N.B. The strict definition of an Issue from the Association for Project Management is that of a problem that cannot be resolved by the Project Manager, and therefore has to be escalated to the Project Sponsor. This book uses a more generic definition of an Issue, and suggests that those Issues which have been escalated to the Project Sponsor are noted as such in the Issue Log.)

Issue Log: A log of all Issues, to be kept up-to-date throughout, thereby providing an audit trail of all problems and their resolution.

IT: Information Technology. Most medium-to-large organisations have an IT department providing technical support to BAU.

KPIs (Key Performance Indicators): Measures of progress towards Success Criteria.

Latest Finish Time: The latest possible time that an activity can finish, given the constraints imposed by successive tasks in the network.

Latest Start Time: The latest possible time that an activity can start, given its Duration and Latest Finish Time.

Lessons Learned Report: A report produced in Closeout which lists all useful lessons learned by the project with the intention of improving projects in the whole organisation.

Negotiation: The process of discussion and bargaining to reach a compromise between two parties.

Network Diagram: A diagram of Nodes, linked by dependencies shown by arrows, used in the calculation of the project duration and critical path. Also known as a precedence network.

Node: The rectangular box in a Network Diagram which holds information about an activity; Earliest and Latest Start and Finish dates and duration.

Norming: The third stage in Tuckman's model of team development.

Operations: The team in the organisation who will ensure the project's products are used and maintained in service to the end users.

Opportunity: A positive risk; the chance that things could go better than we have predicted.

Organisational Breakdown Structure (OBS): A hierarchical structure showing the roles in the project and their reporting lines.

Parametric Estimating: Statistical estimating based on the actual results of the project so far; the most accurate estimating method.

Payback: A simple form of investment appraisal as part of a Business Case. Calculates the time when the project will break even.

Performing: The fourth and final stage in Tuckman's model of team development.

PESTLE: A mnemonic to remember the six areas of a project's context: Political, Economic, Sociological, Technical, Legal and Environmental.

Portfolio: A collection of projects which do not serve the same overall goal, managed as a unit for reasons of convenience.

Post-Project Review: Held after Handover and prior to Closeout, a review of the achievement of the project against what was planned and approved in the Project Management Plan (PMP).

Procurement: The process of acquiring goods or services.

Product: The result of some activity. This includes management products (e.g., the Business Case) or specialist products (e.g., the painted walls).

Product Specification: The complete specification of a product which provides the product developer with a clear definition of what is required, plus the quality measures that will be made against the product when it is quality checked.

Progress Report: A time-based status report to be sent upwards to the next level in the Organisational Breakdown Structure (OBS).

Project Assurance: The organisational role responsible for audit and checking within the project.

Project Board: The organisational group responsible for authorisation and decision-making in the project.

Project Context: The elements of the outside world which may impact on the project.

Project Evaluation Review: An informal review of the project carried out by the Project Manager.

Project Manager: The organisational role responsible for day-to-day management of the project as defined in the Project Management Plan (PMP).

Project Management Plan (PMP): The full and complete project definition that is written by the Project Manager, approved by the Project Board and used as a baseline throughout the project.

Project Plan: The overview of the project, containing the schedule (Gantt chart), and listing objectives, assumptions, milestones, and resource requirements. Should be updated with progress information throughout. Part of the Project Management Plan (PMP).

Project Sponsor: The organisational role responsible for driving the project forward on behalf of the business.

Project Support: The organisational role responsible for the day-to-day administration of the project.

Programme: A collection of projects which serve the same overall goal.

Quality: Meeting the customers' requirements.

Quality Assurance: The function of an organisation responsible for producing and maintaining the Quality Management System (QMS) and for ensuring that all projects are using the Quality Management System (QMS) properly.

Quality Control: The process of checking a product to ensure it meets the required standards; that is, checking it against its Product Specification.

Quality Management System (QMS): The set of processes and standards that an organisation has specified are to be used by every project. It may refer to external standards.

Quality Log: The audit trail of all quality checking work done in the project. Each row in the table will represent the review of one product.

Quality Plan: The project's strategy for delivering the requirements of the customer in accordance with the Quality Management System (QMS).

Resource Histogram: A frequency chart showing the number of resources planned to be used by the project plotted against time.

Resource Levelling: Levelling the Resource Histogram when there is a constraint on the number of resources that can be sued by the project. Also known as resource-limited scheduling. May extend the project timetable.

Resource Smoothing: Smoothing the resource curve by using total float to alter the timing of activities, or adjusting the number of resources per task. Also known as time-limited scheduling, as the project timescale is not extended.

Responsibility Assignment Matrix (RAM): A matrix which joins together the Work Breakdown Structure (WBS) and Organisational Breakdown Structure (OBS) to ensure that every task is assigned to a role.

Risk Analysis: The process of identifying, and assessing project risks, and deciding which actions to use.

Risk Assessment: The evaluation of a risk in terms of probability and impact.

Risk Management: The process of analysing risks and managing them through the project.

Risk Log: The formal register of all project risks, showing their evaluation, actions and current status.

Risk Owner: The person assigned to monitor a risk and report on its status to the Project Manager.

Scope: The sum of work of the project.

Stage: A chunk of the project to be managed at a time, to enable a greater level of planning and control to be exercised.

Stage Boundary: The end of one stage and the start of another; usually separated by management reviews of the project (known as Gate Reviews).

Stage Plan: The plan of a stage. This will have the same contents as, but be more detailed than, the Project Plan.

Stakeholder: Any person or group interested in, or affected by, the project.

Stakeholder Analysis: The process of identifying, then analysing the power and interest of each stakeholder.

Stakeholder Mapping Grid: A diagram to show the power and interest of each stakeholder.

Stakeholder Management: The process of identifying, analysing and deciding actions to influence the views of stakeholders.

Status Accounting: The recording and reporting of data in the configuration database.

Storming: The second stage in Tuckman's model of team development.

Subjective Estimating: The least accurate form of estimate. Performed during Conception to produce a 'ball-park' estimate.

Success Criteria: Measures of the success of the project, either at project closure or afterwards. Different stakeholders will have different success criteria.

Success Factors: Activities or processes that are put into place at the start of the project to enable achievement of the Success Criteria.

Synergy: The combined effect of two or more things to produce an effect greater than the sum of their individual effects.

Team Manager: Organisational role; the person fulfilling it is responsible for day-to-day supervision of team members carrying out project tasks.

Threat: A negative risk; the chance that things could go less well than we have predicted.

Tolerance: The allowed deviation from cost and time budgets without having to involve the next higher level of management.

Total Float: The amount by which an activity can be delayed without affecting the end date of the project.

Work Breakdown Structure (WBS): The hierarchical decomposition of the work in the project into smaller components until individual units of work can be estimated.

Index